Praise for *How Not to Suck at Marketing*

"If you're new to marketing, start here... this incredibly complex discipline to the bare essentials you'll need to market your company and build your personal brand. Thanks to his refreshingly honest stories and humorous anecdotes, you'll find this marketing guide hard to put down."

– Drew Neisser, Founder of Renegade LLC and CMO Huddles, and author of *Renegade Marketing*

"A masterclass in building brands and driving results from a world-class leader, *How Not to Suck at Marketing* is a must read for anyone who loves the art and science of modern marketing."

– Mike Steib, CEO of Artsy and author of *The Career Manifesto*

"Honest, direct, practical, and fun to read. Whether you've just started your career in marketing or are considering executive/c-suite options, you'll find a ton of no-nonsense lessons and perspectives from the trenches... Jeff weaves in both the strategic value of marketing as well as the practical tips needed to be successful (a.k.a. not sucking)."

– Alexandra Gobbi, CMO, Code42 Software

"Authentic, insightful, and entertaining. One of the most difficult aspects of marketing is that everyone – regardless of what they do for a living – thinks they're a marketer and has an opinion about what marketing should do. With his book, Jeff provides the background and blueprint to succeed in the role."

– Jeff Crow, Chief Marketing Officer, Core BTS

"A go-to resource for anyone seeking growth in today's ever-changing business environment. Jeff has written the essential book on how to excel at marketing – while being just an all-around good person to work with."

– Jo Ann Herold, CMO, The Honey Baked Ham Company

"It's no secret that marketing continues to grow more complex... *How Not to Suck at Marketing* provides a playbook – complete with proven tactics that drive impact, insights to help even the most seasoned marketers grow and evolve, and an authentic approach to crafting your own success story."

   – Leigh Segall, Chief Marketing Officer, Smart Communications

"As a finance leader, I view marketing as one of the highest leveraged functions in any organization. Jeff shares real-world examples of how to be successful in scaling a highly effective marketing team that delivers tangible returns on investment. I recommend this book for anyone looking to build an impactful career in marketing."

   – Chad Gold, Chief Financial Officer at SalesLoft

"This sucks! Well, the only thing that sucks is that I didn't have this book earlier in my career. I couldn't stop reading with Jeff's witty humor and breakthrough advice. He takes a complex topic and makes it approachable for anyone who wants to sustain a career in marketing."

   – Kevin OMalley, VP of Account Based Marketing, Gartner

"Jeff takes a realistic approach to 'not sucking' and shares alternative ways to tackle common challenges and frustrating setbacks many marketers face – all in a relatable and inspiring way. A great read for marketers at any stage in their career."

   – Jennifer Zember, VP, Customer Marketing & Brand, SugarCRM

"If you want to accelerate your marketing career, this is the playbook to read. Jeff has a knack for storytelling, so you'll find yourself being entertained as he defines what truly great marketing should look like."

   – Nicole Wojno Smith, VP of Marketing, Tackle.io

HOW 2 CONQUER

HOW NOT TO SUCK AT MARKETING

by Jeff Perkins

HOW 2 CONQUER

Published by How2Conquer
www.how2conquer.com

First edition, September 2021

Edited by Katherine Guntner
Illustrations by Telia Garner
Edited and designed by Emily M. Owens

Library of Congress Control Number: 2021942264

Print ISBN 978-1-945783-15-9
Ebook ISBN 978-1-945783-16-6

For Mia and Ella

and

In memory of my friend, Ian Crystal.
A brilliant marketing mind
gone too soon.

CONTENTS

Introduction 1

Part 1: Why You Suck at Marketing 3
You Suck 4
The Good Old Days 5
The Rise of Internet Advertising 6
The New Normal for Marketers 7
Company Brand vs Personal Brand 9
Is Marketing at Risk? 11

Part 2: How Not to Suck 15
The Basics 16
Two Essential Skills for Modern Marketers 20
Using Core Values to Nurture Your Company Brand 26
Don't Let Your Brand Be That Guy 31
What Your Tagline Says About Your Brand 33
Finding the Watering Holes 35
Always Be Testing 37
Creating Raving Fans 40

Part 3: Having a Career That Doesn't Suck 47
Career Basics 48
Building a Flexible and Focused Career 67
Play Nice with Others 81
Navigate Job Changes 87

Part 4: Assemble a Bigger & Better Band 93
Better Together 94
Playing Nice 103

Part 5: Avoid Sucking at Small Business
Marketing 119
Becoming Your Own CMO 120
Taking It to The Next Level 129

Part 6: Crisis Does Suck, But You Can Thrive 137
Marketing in the Time of COVID................................138

Part 7: Marketing Lessons as Memoir 149
My Career...150
Unfocused Beginnings..150
Hello, Saatchi & Saatchi.......................................152
The MBA: An Opportunity to Learn
   How Not to Suck 160
Post-MBA Career...165
NYC to OMD to GSK..167
AutoTrader...175
PGi: A Key "Sucking Less" Story..........................178
QASymphony: A CMO Rocket................................179
The ParkMobile Opportunity 181
And another thing 185

Epilogue: The TAG Marketing Awards 187

Resources 191
Marketing Resources 192
Glossary of Marketing Acronyms.........................197
Acknowledgements..201
About the Author..202

INTRODUCTION

I stood in the bathroom for several minutes staring at the anguished expression on my face in the mirror.

I had been in my current job for six months. When I first started, I saw so much opportunity for improvement. I mean, the bar was very low. The brand was a mess. The website was a disaster. Our presence on search engines was non-existent. From a marketing perspective, we were doing everything wrong that you could possibly do wrong.

When I started the job, I thought to myself, "Man, I am going to absolutely crush it." But here I was six months later, and I hadn't made much progress. It wasn't that I wasn't working hard or didn't know what to do. I just wasn't making the progress I needed to make. I wasn't moving fast enough. And after six months, I couldn't just blame the previous marketing team. This was my mess now. I owned it.

Before I left the bathroom, I looked at myself one more time, shook my head, and blurted out, "You suck."

PART 1:
WHY YOU SUCK AT MARKETING

You Suck

The feeling of "sucking" at your job is just horrible, but I've found that it is all too common for many marketers.

I was speaking at the Digital Summit in Atlanta, GA a few years back. The title for my session was "How Not to Suck at Marketing." I thought it would be a catchy title. Digital Summit is one of those conferences where there are always 3–4 different sessions going on at the same time, so having a good title is key to getting a big audience.

But I wasn't prepared for how many people showed up for my session. It was totally packed – standing room only – and some people were even sitting on the floor.

I started the presentation by saying, "Welcome, I guess this is a support group for marketers who suck." It got a big laugh. But the best humor is always grounded in some truth. And the truth is, a lot of us do suck at our jobs.

It's understandable. Marketing today is very hard; it's increasingly complex and always changing. Just look at Scott Brinker's annual Martech Landscape Chart[1], which shows the

---

1. Find Scott Brinker's Martech Landscape Chart at chiefmartech.com.

8000+ different tools a marketer can use today. That's right, over 8000!

I've been watching this chart grow for many years. Back in 2011, there were only about 150 martech tools on the list. Now you can't even look at it without a magnifying glass. As a marketer, which tools do you absolutely need, and which ones are just nice to haves? How do you prioritize? Where do you even start when it comes to an evaluation process?

It's just overwhelming and a good example of why being a marketer today is a big challenge.

But it hasn't always been this way.

The Good Old Days

When I started my career in the mid-1990s, I worked for a big ad agency in New York City – Saatchi & Saatchi. My client was Procter & Gamble, and I worked on the Tide and Cascade brands. I always thought it was funny that I lived in a tiny NYC apartment without a dishwasher or washer/dryer, yet I did the advertising for the biggest dish and laundry detergent brands in the world. (For more about my experiences as a young ad executive, see **"Part 7: Marketing Lessons as Memoir" on page 149**.)

Back in the '90s, advertising was much simpler. If you wanted to do an ad, you really only had a few options – print, TV, radio, or outdoor. The internet as we know it today was just emerging. There was no Google, just a random assortment of now-defunct search engines like Alta Vista, Web Crawler, Excite, and HotBot. There really wasn't much online advertising at all.

Making decisions about where to advertise was relatively easy. It was really all about the 30-second TV spot. At the agency, we would joke that you would say to the client, "The answer is a 30-second spot, now tell me what your business problem is."

There was a truth to that. I remember we would spend most of our time debating each individual frame of a storyboard and each word in the copy. Then we would present it to the client, and we would debate some more. Then we would move on to the qualitative testing, then the quantitative testing. Finally, we would have a spot that we would produce. After we filmed it, we would do another round of research before it would air on TV. It was a lot of work to get a 30-second spot on the air.

In a given year, we might have done four TV ads. That was all we did for 12 months. 120 seconds of video to promote a brand. Looking back now, it almost seems impossible that you would accomplish so little over that time period. But that was just how things worked.

The Rise of Internet Advertising

Then in the late '90s, internet advertising started to emerge. It was totally different from anything I had done before. Instead of spending months researching every single aspect of a TV ad, we would just throw stuff online and see how it performed. We'd see one banner got more clicks than another, so we'd remove the banner that was underperforming.

What an amazing time it was to be a marketer! We'd test concepts and messaging in real-time, with real customers, then optimize on the fly! We felt like we were the rulers of this new marketing world.

I remember doing digital advertising for the merger of ExxonMobil in 1998. They were mostly doing TV and print ads for the campaign, but they decided to throw a "little" money into digital. They were planning to spend just a few million dollars online, about 2% of the total campaign budget – but at the time, there was so little internet advertising spend that we basically owned the internet. There wasn't that much inventory, so you couldn't go to a site without seeing an ExxonMobil banner.

From those humble beginnings, digital advertising started to consume everything. It changed the way marketers would allocate budget. It even changed our vernacular, as everything in the digital world seems to be an acronym – CPC, CPA, CTR, KPI, CLV, SQL, LTV, MQL, PPC, SEO, SEM, VTC, CPL, CTA, RTB, ROS, RON… Modern marketers can basically speak in complete sentences using only acronyms. When I look at all these acronyms, all I can say is "WTF." (Make sure to check out the **"Glossary of Marketing Acronyms" on page 197**).

The New Normal for Marketers

While this new wave of digital advertising created a great opportunity for marketers to be more effective and accountable, it has also created significant challenges. Today the pressure on marketing is greater than ever because there is a belief held by many executives that all marketing investments should be clearly measurable. You need to show an immediate ROI on every single penny spent.

This is a significant shift for many marketers who grew up hearing John Wanamaker's famous quote, "Half the money I spend on advertising is wasted; the trouble is, I don't know which half." It's not that marketers don't want accountability, but the idea that you will be measured and judged for everything you do is a pretty scary prospect.

You basically have these two competing forces at play:

» **Brand Awareness:** The act of building a brand over time. Requires a sustained investment and a focus on consistency for many years.
» **Immediate ROI:** The need to show an immediate return on your marketing investment. Requires constant testing and optimization in real-time.

In my experience, marketing has always been about the long game. You don't spend money now to drive an immediate result. Rather, it's about sustained investment over time. It's about building awareness and interest. And in most cases, you can't do that overnight.

Therein lies the trap for the modern marketer. You have all these new digital tactics you can use to track immediate results. But effective marketing has always required patience. Imagine if Nike ran a few print ads with the "Just Do It" tagline and shoe sales didn't immediately go up. Would Phil Knight have pulled all of the marketing budget? No. That's why "Just Do It" is one of the most memorable taglines in history. It's been around for over 30 years!

The old rules of marketing are still valid. Brands take time and money to build. But in a world where you can track everything, and CEOs and boards are looking for immediate returns, it's getting harder and harder for marketers to make that case.

BRAND AWARENESS:
- The act of building a brand over time.
- Requires a sustained investment and a focus on consistency for many years.

IMMEDIATE R.O.I.
- The need to show an immediate return on your marketing investment.
- Requires constant testing + optimization in real-time.

Company Brand vs Personal Brand

One of the other challenges for modern marketers is that your job today is not just about building the brand for your company. You also have to spend time on your personal brand.

What does this mean? Well, it means that you have to define what your personal brand is, and then make sure you're actively managing that brand.

Some of you might say, "Jeff, doing a good job and driving results for my company *is* my personal brand."

That's a fair point. But I would ask you this: How will people outside your company know that you're doing a good job? Without a strong personal brand, the truth is, they probably won't.

Saatchi & Saatchi built a strong reputation as a company that did effective ad campaigns for Fortune 500 companies like Procter & Gamble, General Mills, Johnson & Johnson, Delta Airlines, and more. So if an enterprise company was looking for a new agency, Saatchi & Saatchi would usually be on the shortlist.

I later went to work at an agency called Kirshenbaum, Bond & Partners.[2] Now, this agency was much different. It was smaller and more creative. They positioned themselves as a "word of mouth" agency, meaning they would do highly creative and unconventional ad campaigns that would create a lot of buzz. They famously did ads for a lingerie brand with street stencils that said, "From here, it looks like you could use some new underwear." Companies looking for an inventive, buzzworthy campaign would put Kirshenbaum, Bond & Partners on the shortlist.

Both Saatchi & Saatchi and KB&P built strong corporate brands that would attract the right kind of clients for them.

---

2. I recommend reading Richard Kirshenbaum and Jon Bond's book *Under the Radar: Talking to Today's Cynical Consumers.* Many of the lessons are still highly relevant to modern marketers.

Similarly, modern marketers need to think about how to position themselves. Are you a B2B marketer or a B2C marketer? Are you better suited for a large company or a startup? Are you a social media expert? Can you build Adwords campaigns? Have you implemented a marketing automation solution? Have you managed large teams?

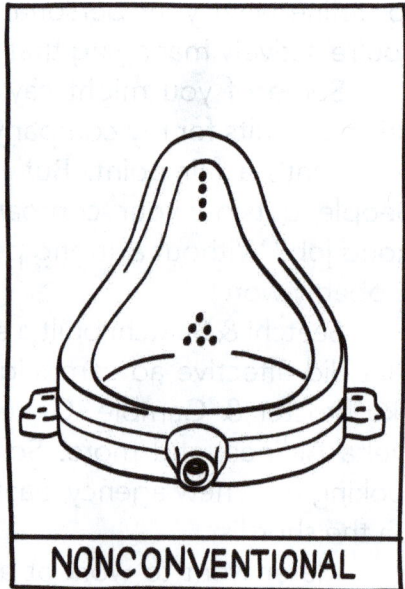

| ENTERPRISE | NONCONVENTIONAL |

Answering these types of questions will help you define your personal brand. Once you do, part of your job is to continue building your brand, making sure people understand how you as a marketing professional are positioned compared to your peers – so when the right opportunity opens up, you'll be on the shortlist.

We'll explore building your personal brand in much more depth in **Part 3: Having a Career That Doesn't Suck**. This is an important topic, because the truth is that all marketers today are at risk.

Is Marketing at Risk?

I've worked at several companies in the past few years where marketing has been literally blown up every few months.

The CEO of one of my previous employers once told me that "nothing was working, so he fired the marketing department." You read that right. He "fired the marketing department" – and this wasn't a small department. This was a department of 50+ people who were walked out the door. The CEO wasn't seeing the results he wanted, so he decided to blow the whole thing up.

The last company I worked for, QASymphony (now called Tricentis), had four marketing leaders from 2013–2015 before I joined. That's right: four marketing leaders in two years. Luckily for me, I lasted much longer than my predecessors. And at my current job at ParkMobile, the previous CMO was in and out in six months.

But why? Why have I had success where others have failed? It's not because I'm smarter, or more experienced, or a better marketer. More than anything, I believe that it probably has to do with my mindset when it comes to marketing and my approach to the job.

In the following chapters, I'll provide some practical advice on how to be a better marketer, how to build a great marketing team, and how to strengthen relationships between marketing and other departments. Hopefully, some of this might prevent you from getting fired, but I offer no guarantees. I'll also provide some tips on how to build a career in marketing that doesn't suck.

Are you in? Let's get started.

KEY TAKEAWAYS:

» Marketing has grown increasingly complex over the past decades with the introduction of digital advertising and an array of new marketing technologies.

» The rapid changes in the industry have left some marketers behind and others struggling to keep up with the constant change. That's why the CMO usually has the shortest tenure in the C-suite.

» Modern marketers have to figure out the right mix of longer-term tactics that build brand awareness and short-term programs that drive results now.

» In this constantly changing industry where marketing professionals are constantly at risk of losing their jobs, having a strong personal brand becomes a necessity.

PART 2:
HOW NOT TO SUCK

The Basics

Pouring a Strong Foundation

In my role, I get to attend a lot of marketing conferences. As marketers, we love conferences. Whether you're a B2B or B2C marketer, we can find any and every excuse to attend a conference. Sometimes, I think marketers spend more time at conferences than doing actual work.

Note: One of the funny things I've noticed at industry events is what seems to be the "official digital marketer uniform" for guys – jeans and a blazer. I'm serious. Go to any marketing conference and every dude is wearing jeans and a blazer. I guess that's the new suit and tie. So if you're a guy just starting your marketing career and it's your first day of work, invest in some nice denim and a few quality blazers and shirts to look the part. Same advice for all new marketers – invest in quality basics. But I'm pretty sure you don't want more fashion advice than that from me.

At these conferences, there are a lot of shiny objects: people talking about cool next-gen marketing topics related to the Internet of Things (IoT), the latest social media platform, artificial intelligence, etc. But often these conferences lack any discussion of the basics. Basics are just not sexy.

But here's the interesting thing: how many people at these conferences are actually doing the basics right? How many have strong websites and rank on page one of Google for all the strategic search terms relevant to their business?

The truth is that most marketers are still struggling with the basics. They're not even close to being ready for the more advanced stuff.

When I've presented at these conferences before, I've

actually been asked questions like "What's PPC?" or "What's a bounce rate?" That's not a bad thing, and I'm glad the attendees asked. There were probably a lot of other people in the audience with the exact same questions who were too shy to raise their hands.

Here's the reality for marketers today. You have to do the basics right before you do anything else.

What Are the Basics?

In today's competitive marketplace, customers are harder to reach than ever before. The old sales methods of using brute force cold calling are over. Think about it, when was the last time you answered a call on your phone when you didn't recognize the number? I mean, I don't even answer the phone when I know the person calling. So, if I don't know your number, you don't have a chance. When was the last time you replied to a cold email other than to ask the sender to please take you off their list? And don't even get me started on LinkedIn. It has gotten to the point where almost 90% of my invitation requests are from people trying to sell me something. There's really nothing worse than accepting a LinkedIn invite and then immediately getting a sales pitch.

Today, customers are in control. Customers will evaluate your products or services on their terms and on their time. And when they're ready, they will reach out to you. Studies show that most buyers are 70%–80% through the buying process before they even talk to a sales rep. What does this mean for marketers? We have to absolutely obsess over what customers are doing during that 70%–80% of their evaluation time.

And what are they doing? Well, it probably varies by category or industry. But according to the studies I've read, the majority of buyers are using search engines and visiting vendor websites. If your search engine presence is lacking and your website is bad, you are going to have a hard time attracting customers.

The two basics are:

1. A good website
2. A strong search engine presence

These are key to attracting customers to your product.

The Virtual Sales Rep

Let's think about it another way. In the past, the first interaction many prospects would have with a potential vendor was through the sales rep. Today that dynamic has flipped. The interaction with the sales rep comes much later in the process. Instead, prospects are first interacting with what I would call the "virtual sales rep" – a search engine and your website. And if you aren't focused on making that interaction a positive one, you're probably losing deals you don't even know about.

When I was CMO of QASymphony, I spent a lot of time talking to our customers right after they bought our product. The first question I always asked was how they found out about us. The answer almost always went something like this:

"Well, we were interested in getting a new software tool, so we decided to evaluate a few options. We did some Google searches, and you guys kept coming up. So we did some research on your website, and you made the shortlist."

So when I talk about "the basics," I'm really talking about your website and your search engine presence. Marketers today have to make sure those two areas are very strong because if you're weak online, you'll be weak offline.

Fortunately, there are plenty of tools out there to help you access the strength of your website and search engine presence. Here are a few you should check out:

» Moz is a great tool for search engine optimization. It shows how you rank for your strategic keywords and compares you to the competition.

» Hubspot has a "website grader" that gives you a free diagnostic of your website and free tips for improvement.

» Crazy Egg shows you a visual heatmap of website interactions. This helps you understand what people are doing on your site.

» Usertesting.com is a great resource that lets you get real user feedback on your site so you can understand what's working and what's not.

» Google Analytics will give you a ton of metrics to help you improve the performance of your website.

As marketers, we have to make sure when buyers are out there doing that research and making critical decisions, our brands are highly visible.

So how do you achieve the necessary visibility to make the shortlist of an evaluation? Well, it's not that complicated.

1. Rank on page one of Google for the terms the buyer would be searching for. At QASymphony, most were searching for "software testing tools" or "test case management tools." We made sure we were ranking organically for those terms, and we would also buy those key terms to improve our prominence on the page.

2. Have a presence on other sites that compile lists of solutions for your category. At QASymphony, we would get a lot of referral leads from websites with lists of the "Top Software Testing Tools." I'll talk more about this topic in **"Finding the Watering Holes" on page 35**.

3. When you get prospects to your website, make sure you are providing content that will convince them that you are a company worth considering. This includes mentions of current clients, industry accolades, and

impressive stats. The goal is that your prospect takes one look at your homepage and says, "Well, we're definitely putting this company on the shortlist."

4. Show the product. Your website should be full of videos – demos that show the product in action. Even better, offer a free trial so your prospects can kick the tires before reaching out to a sales rep.

There's a lot more that goes into all of this. But if you are doing these four things right, you will generate a lot of "at bats" for your sales teams.

Two Essential Skills for Modern Marketers

I speak to a lot of college and graduate students about careers in marketing. A common question I get is: "What are the essential skills I need coming out of school?"

Students are looking for direction on what they should study or what classes they should take. Should they focus on learning about brand management, market research, communications, or analytics?

I usually give a different kind of answer to that question. I think there are two key skills modern marketers need to be successful: flexibility and focus. This is probably an unconventional answer for some. Let me explain.

The most successful marketers today will be able to:

1. Have the flexibility to constantly course correct as things change and evolve over time.
2. Avoid the shiny objects and focus on fewer things that will make the biggest impact to the business.

Learn to be Flexible

I've worked with a lot of different marketing professionals in my career – some good, some bad. One thing I've always noticed is that the best marketers are very flexible. They understand there are many ways to solve the same problem.

They are quick to change course if something doesn't work. They don't dwell on past mistakes. They move on fast.

On the other hand, I've found that some of the less successful marketers are the most rigid. They believe there's a "right way" to do marketing, and they have a hard time deviating from that path. "Trust the process," they will tell you.

These are the people who strictly adhere to the classic marketing frameworks taught in business school and at conferences. Even when something isn't working, they cling to the belief that it will eventually work. It has to. You just have to give it more time.

They might actually be right about that. I've found that executives are often too impatient when it comes to marketing initiatives. They want results, and they want them now.

The problem is that the rigid marketer lacks self-awareness. They can't see that the business doesn't have time to wait. They may say, "My CEO just doesn't get it."

Well, do you know what your CEO gets? He gets that he will be fired if your company misses its number. If you're not helping him hit that number, you're just overhead. And that's probably why the CMO has the shortest tenure in the C-suite – this book could just have easily been titled *How Not to Get Fired by the CEO*.

The Importance of Focus

A common pitfall marketers encounter when they first join a company is the desire to do too much too soon. It's like you're a kid in a candy store. There's just so much opportunity to make a difference and show your stuff. It's always fun to point out areas where the prior team "got it wrong" and tell everyone how you're going to fix it all.

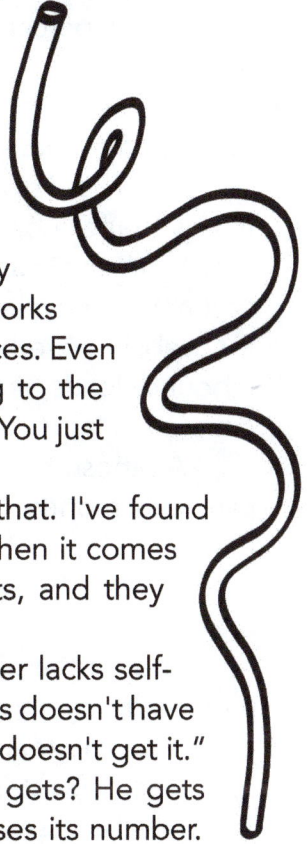

That's where you can get yourself in serious trouble. If you try to do too many things at once, you probably won't end up getting much done. If you aren't getting much done, there might be a perception that you're ineffective. And if you get labeled ineffective, that's when the wheels start coming off.

I've seen this happen many times in my career. A new marketing leader joins the company, and everyone is super excited. The new marketing leader has BIG plans to fix things that are broken, implement new programs, and drive results for the company. The new marketing leader decides to immediately embark on a rebranding initiative, rebuild the website, overhaul the messaging, improve SEO, increase inbound leads, implement a new analytics platform, and organize a large user conference.

All those tactics I just listed are huge undertakings that can take months or even years to complete. But the new marketing leader thinks he or she can do it all. The marketing leader makes big promises to the team, the executives, and the board.

Then a few weeks go by and nothing happens. A few months go by and the marketer still isn't making meaningful progress. The team starts losing patience with the marketer. The executives start wondering if they hired the right person. The board isn't seeing the numbers they want from marketing.

Eventually, that marketing leader gets fired or relegated to a smaller role within the team. Then a new marketing leader is hired, and the cycle begins all over again.

> Here's the key point marketers must remember: You can do anything. But you can't do everything.

Marketers need to focus. You can't fix everything at once. Choosing what *not* to do is just as important as choosing what to do. But in any organization, there are a million things that need to get done. How do you possibly decide what to focus on?

There's no right answer, but here's an approach I use for figuring it out. On a piece of paper, write down these statements:

» We are not growing revenue faster because

_____.

» We are losing deals because

_____.

Fill in the blanks, and that should tell you where to focus your efforts. Everything else can probably wait.

For example, your answers might look something like:

» We are not growing revenue faster because **of a lack of awareness in the industry**.
» We are losing deals because **we are missing an important product feature**.

In this case, for the first statement, you will want to focus your efforts on doing everything you can to build that awareness. Maybe you need to start going to more industry trade shows and buying ads in key print and digital trade publications. For the second fill-in-the-blank statement, you'll need to work closely with the product team to make sure they understand the importance of that missing feature and get it on the roadmap. You'll also need to help your sales team with messaging to overcome any objections related to that missing feature.

When I started at QASymphony, there was a lot of work that had to be done. We were a startup that had just raised a Series A[3], so we didn't have a lot of the foundational pieces

---

3. A Series A is a company's first significant round of venture capital financing.

in place. I could have spent a lot of time building collateral, working on messaging, and overhauling the brand. But when I filled in the blanks in the statements above, the answer was simple: we did not have enough leads for the sales team.

As a startup, we needed revenue and we needed it now. That means lead generation became my #1 priority.

I tried to avoid any project that wasn't focused on driving leads for the sales team. My first hire was a Director of Demand Generation. I reallocated as much budget as I could into driving leads, which meant firing our PR agency and putting those dollars into lead generating-focused tactics.

After a month, we started seeing a significant increase in leads. The sales team was happy. My CEO was happy. That bought me some much-needed goodwill and credibility, which would help as I took on bigger projects that would fill some of the foundational gaps in our marketing program.

For marketing leaders, focus is key. It's better to do a few key things very well than a lot of things poorly.

We are not growing revenue faster because of _a lack of awareness in the industry._

We are losing deals because _we are missing an important product feature._

The Quick Win Strategy

It's not just about being focused; it's also about choosing the right things to focus on. One of the key factors you need to consider when selecting your areas of focus is how big or small a project is. How long will it take? Because if you focus on one big program that takes too long to execute, you could be in trouble.

From 2012 to 2015, I worked at a technology company called PGi. After about 18 months into the job, I really felt I was hitting my stride and doing some good work. One day, a colleague from the finance department came up to me and said, "You've really accomplished a lot since you've been at the company." I was flattered. That's a really nice complement. I'm usually not one to celebrate victories because I'm focused on the next game.

Looking back at that year and a half at PGi, my team did accomplish a lot. We launched a new global corporate website and made some significant improvements to our online marketing program. Our metrics were improving on a weekly basis. We'd built a sales channel that was generating over $200,000 in monthly recurring revenue and growing at double digits. Most importantly, I brought on some great new team members who were helping get us to where we wanted to be.

Taking an inventory of your accomplishments really forces you to look back and evaluate the choices you've made on what to do and where to focus your time and resources.

If you try to take on too many areas for improvement at once – what I call a "boil the ocean" strategy – the results usually aren't very good. You end up spending too little time on too many things. The outcome is that nothing actually gets done.

I prefer a "quick win" strategy. Find one thing that you can do that won't take months or years to complete and just go after it. Do it really well and show the results. Then go on to the next quick win and repeat the process all over again.

After a while, you'll start to show some real progress as a bunch of small quick wins start to add up. You'll also gain a reputation as someone who gets stuff done, and in any organization, being perceived as "effective" can really help your career. The next time that special "CEO project" comes up, you just might get tapped to run it based on your track record.

Also, building up street cred with your quick wins will eventually help you when you're ready to take on some of the bigger, longer-term, and more ambitious projects. Your management and peers will have more faith that you can get it done and it won't be one of those projects that seems to go on forever.

So when you're looking at all the projects on your overflowing plate, just think about how to break them up into smaller, quick wins that you can get done now.

> Just like in baseball, the team that consistently put runs on the board usually beats the team that lives and dies by the home run.

Using Core Values to Nurture Your Company Brand

You might start reading this chapter thinking, "Jeff, what do the company's core values have to do with marketing?"

I'd say they have everything to do with marketing. Your brand has to be built on a strong foundation. If you don't have clearly defined core values, that foundation will be shaky.

At my last two companies, we did not have core values when I joined, and it was one of the first projects I took on. Why? Because it's hard to build a brand if you don't understand who you are. That's what core values help you define. And it's hard for employees to really get behind the company if they don't understand what its values are.

If you are a fitness enthusiast like me, you've probably read about the importance of having a strong core. The core of your body is foundational to your overall physical fitness. While it's nice to have big quads or toned biceps, the core is critical because it provides total body strength and prevents injuries.

I look at a company's core values the same way. When you define them, you're working on your core. You're building strength that will help everything you do.

Defining Your Core Values

How do you create core values for your company? Well, there's no secret sauce.

First, you pick a group of people. I've found that it's good to get a diverse group with different perspectives who are all passionate about the company. This group should spend time together and talk about both the values that are important to them as individuals and to the company as a whole.

Here are some of the key questions you should ask when you're developing your core values:

1. What is important to our company?
2. How do we treat each other?
3. How do we treat our customers?
4. What is unique about us?
5. How do we work together?
6. What is the best thing about working here?
7. What is different about our company compared to others?
8. What word or words would you use to describe the people at the company?

Another useful exercise during a core values work session is to have people share some experiences they've had while working at the company. Then discuss what values you can derive from those stories.

For example, during our ParkMobile work session, there was a lot of conversation about how people at the

company constantly go above and beyond to support each other. People from different departments will often jump in and lend a hand when needed. It was not uncommon for people from the finance department to help complete Quality Assurance (QA)[4] testing for a new product release if we needed the extra help to hit our deadlines. This ended up being translated into our core value – "Rise and Fall Together."

After you finish the whiteboard session, you'll need someone who can translate that conversation into words on a page. As the marketing and communications person, this responsibility usually falls to me. I take the first stab at writing down our core values and then circulate it around the group. People make comments and suggest edits to the document, then we finalize it.

The creation process usually only takes a few weeks if you focus and make it a priority.

A few rules I've learned in creating core values:

1. Limit the number of core values: You will probably have a long list of core values, but you really need to narrow it down to anywhere from four to eight.
2. Keep it simple: Each core value should be a word or short statement. You want people in the company to be able to remember them, so it can't be too long.
3. Briefly explain what each core value means: It's good to have a short explainer to help reinforce the meaning.

---

4. Quality Assurance focuses on the project process and design of a product to prevent defects or safety issues. Quality Control (QC) identifies any of these issues or defects in a product at each iteration. QA and QC are often used interchangeably but differ slightly.

Example: ParkMobile Core Values

» **A Healthy Obsession with the Customer Experience:** Our goal is simple: create raving fans. From our app and online tools to our customer service team, we are determined to make every interaction with ParkMobile and our products perfect.

» **Act with Integrity:** Relationships are built on trust, not tricks. We always want to win, but only if we can win the right way. We own our commitments and are accountable. We hold ourselves to a higher standard.

» **Sweat the Small Stuff:** The details matter, and we are not afraid to roll up our sleeves and get into the weeds. We know that good enough is never enough. We make sure that the job is done right, and we don't rest until it is.

» **Play Well with Others:** We are just one piece of the puzzle; we must be able to connect with the other pieces to realize our vision. We pride ourselves on being a partner that collaborates with everyone and is easy to work with.

» **Rise and Fall Together:** We are one team. We work hard. We are accountable for our actions and to each other. We win together. We lose together. We stay together.

» **Support Our People, Support Our Community:** We know that our people are our most important asset. We strive to invest in and take care of our people and contribute to the communities where we live.

Instilling Core Values into the Company Culture

Establishing your core values is just the beginning of the journey. Now you have to figure out how those values will integrate into business. A good first step is to thoroughly educate employees on the new core values – really explain the meaning of each one. It's always good to have the CEO or other executives do this at a company meeting.

Then you have to continually reinforce the importance of the core values to the organization. At ParkMobile, we put them on the walls throughout the office. Every employee is given a nice collateral piece they can hang at their desk.

We've also made our core values a key part of how we operate. We use them as a tool to evaluate potential job candidates as well as in our employee performance reviews. We use them to determine who we hire, who we fire, who gets promoted, who gets bonuses, and more. Employees who don't align well with our core values usually don't last long at the company.

My personal favorite way we promote our core values is at our annual company holiday party, where we do "Core Values Awards" recognizing employees who truly embody each core value. These employees are nominated and voted on by their peers. When each employee comes up to accept the award, our CEO thoroughly explains why that person won.

Today, I think most employees at ParkMobile can recite most of the core values off the top of their head. That's when you know you've done a good job integrating core values into your culture.

Recently, I was interviewing a candidate for a position on my team. I asked her why she wanted to work at ParkMobile. Without hesitation she said, "I was reading about your core values, and I really connected with them." We ended up hiring her, and she has been a total rock star for our team.

Before you start thinking about your overall marketing program, make sure your company has strong core values that are well defined and understood by the organization. That's the strong foundation you need to build your brand.

Don't Let Your Brand Be That Guy

Now that we have strong core values established, let's move on to your brand.

As you're thinking through your overall marketing program, it's important to focus on the brand. In our digital world, there might be a tendency to focus on the array of KPIs to track business success. But if you don't spend time nurturing your brand, it could really drag you down. On the flip side, a strong brand that connects with your target audience can improve all your marketing metrics. Let me explain what I'm talking about.

A few years back, I worked with this guy who had a very healthy ego. For the purposes of this book, let's call him Bob. Well, Bob would just go on and on about how great he was. He had an MBA from a top business school. He had great work experience. He had worked internationally. He wore custom-made suits. He chatted with the CEO daily. He had a hot wife. And on and on and on.

Does this guy sound familiar? I think every office has a Bob. Or as I call him, "That Guy." You know him – the one who is offensively arrogant, and at the same time lacks all self-awareness of how others perceive him.

I actually didn't think Bob was a bad guy. He was pretty smart if you could get past his constant chest beating. And he was good at his job. But everyone hated Bob. Why? Because he was just too full of himself.

You're probably thinking, how does this relate to marketing? Well, brands are just like people. It's very important to pay attention to your "brand personality." Who is your brand? What are they like? Would you want to sit next to your brand on a six-hour flight? These are interesting questions for a marketer to ask.

This was exactly what we grappled with back when I worked at AutoTrader.com. Our company had gone from a small dotcom to an industry leader in just nine years. We were very proud of our achievements, and we were not bashful about promoting our success.

Our B2B advertising campaign at the time reflected this celebration of success. We weren't at all modest when it came to telling our customers how great we were. Our tagline at the time was "What We Do Works." All of our advertising featured big claims about how good we were.

A wake-up call came when we showed some of our ads to our customers in a focus group. The moderator asked the group, "What's the first thing that you think when you see these ads?"

"Arrogant!" said one customer.

"It's all about you. But what about your customers?" said yet another.

As I sat behind the double glass watching this unfold, I thought back to Bob. Oh my God, I thought, our brand is "That Guy."

It was a sobering realization. But once we accepted reality, we sought to change it. The first step was to make sure our customers understood the most important thing:

We are only successful if they are successful.

We had to take a humbler approach to our marketing. Instead of talking about ourselves in our trade advertising, we talked about our customers and demonstrated how our partnership produced positive results for their business.

We also changed our advertising tagline to "We Work for You" – a small change in words but a big change in meaning.

So, what happened? Our ads started to resonate more with our audience. In fact, our ads consistently ranked in the top five when we did print ad testing. I don't say that to brag. Well, maybe just a little bit. Old habits die hard.

A few years after we launched the campaign, we did more focus groups. This time around, our customers didn't look at our ads with that "I-just-drank-sour-milk" look on their faces. Instead, they responded positively. When the focus group moderator asked for their first impression of our new and more humble ads, a dealer responded: "Partnership."

Now, that's what we were looking for!

Brands are like people. They have distinct personalities. Ask yourself as a marketer, what's your brand's personality? Is that personality going to win over your customers or turn them off?

Take it from me: people want to work with people they like. And people want to buy brands they like.

So, is your brand likeable? Or is your brand "That Guy?"

What Your Tagline Says About Your Brand

Beyond brand personality, let's talk about taglines. The corporate tagline is an often overlooked and underappreciated part of a brand's messaging.

Some brands have had the same tagline forever. Other brands seem to change the tagline every year. Some brands have multiple taglines. Others have no tagline at all.

There isn't universal agreement on what a tagline is or what role it plays in a brand's marketing. Personally, I believe the tagline is critical. At best, it should be the most concise articulation of your value to your customers. When I was at PGi, we went through an exploratory exercise which led to a new tagline. Let's explore some of the thinking behind it.

For several years, PGi was using the tagline: **The Meeting Experts.**

It's not a bad tagline. It clearly highlighted our expertise and experience in the virtual meeting business. For customers evaluating PGi as a potential vendor, the tagline literally positioned us as "experts" in what we do.

For me, it lacked something. I think the main thing that bothered me was that the tagline was more about us than our customers. Proclaiming that we were "experts" felt a little bit like chest beating.

How Not to Suck at Marketing

Think about it this way: If you were at a party and someone walked around telling everyone they were an "expert," you'd probably say, "That guy is an asshole." It's always better for other people to call you an expert rather than proclaiming it about yourself.

We started our exploratory exercise by interviewing our key executives, including our CEO. We talked to them about the history of the company, the value to our customers, and what made us special. As I conducted the interviews, one message came through loud and clear:

PGi is focused on giving our customers a strategic advantage by improving their ability to communicate and collaborate when they are not actually together in an office.

That was a very interesting message – much different from "The Meeting Experts," and a much bigger story about the value we brought to our customers.

We started to work on new taglines. We had a range of ideas, but the concept that kept sticking with me was this idea of giving our customers a "competitive advantage." We wrote that up on the white board and started iterating around it. Very quickly, we landed on the tagline: **Collaborative Advantage**.

There's something clever yet compelling about it. It's a nice play on the term "competitive advantage," yet it was true to our core. And it wasn't about us. It was about the value we provided to our customers.

We launched the tagline in Q4 of 2013, and it quickly became part of our corporate vernacular. It was on email signatures, business cards, and marketing materials. In an earnings call, our CEO even weaved it into his statement.

It's not every day you get to develop a new tagline for your company. I'm grateful that the PGi executive team gave me the green light to change the corporate tagline. The company has had a lot of changes in recent years, so that tagline is no longer in use, but it's still one of my favorites.

If you're thinking about changing your brand's tagline, take a deep look inside your organization. Try to find the true soul of your brand. What makes you special? Then find the few words to tell that story.

Finding the Watering Holes

Paid advertising can be super expensive. In any category you operate in, there's usually going to be one company that just spends crazy amounts of money to be everywhere – search engines, social channels, video platforms, etc. The tendency for competitors is to just follow the leader; try to match and exceed that marketing spend to compete.

I remember talking to one competitor at a conference and commenting that I see his ads everywhere. "Yeah, we spend big on advertising," he said. "If we cut our ad spend back, we'd actually be profitable."

I thought that was an interesting comment. Clearly, advertising was a key part of this company's growth strategy. The investors were okay with the company losing money in the short term to grow and acquire market share. But not every investor will just let you burn cash on big ad campaigns. In fact, many will want to minimize the marketing spend as much as possible, unless you can show a clear ROI on every dollar spent.

When I joined QASymphony, it was a startup company, and we didn't have much money to spend on advertising. We had recently raised a Series A of about $2 million and needed most of that cash to run the business and scale our operations. So, as a marketing leader, what do you do if you have a very limited budget?

Well, in this case we wanted to be highly targeted with any investments we were making. There wasn't much room for error, so we spent a lot of time trying to figure out the most efficient places we could reach our users and make the biggest impact. How do you do this?

The first step was talking to some of our recently acquired customers to find out how they had learned about us. All the clients I spoke with said basically the same thing:

they had used the "virtual sales rep" method I talked about in The Basics chapter. They'd spent time Googling "best software testing tools" and read a few articles from the first page of the search results. These articles had titles like "20 Best Software Testing Solutions" and "50 Top Test Case Management Tools." The clients then built a shortlist based on those lists.

I refer to these kinds of sites as "watering holes," meaning that they are places your target audience gathers to get information and stay up to date on the latest industry trends. Watering holes can be key to efficiently reaching and influencing your audience.

Fortunately for QASymphony, we were already on all the lists at these watering holes – but we were pretty far down the page. Our key competitors were all ranked higher than we were, but if we could improve our position on these lists, I thought we could increase our inbound lead volume significantly. We started reaching out directly to these sites, asking how we could move up the page.

Initially, I'd thought these rankings were actually based on a thorough independent analysis. I quickly learned it was actually much more random than that. When we talked to the website publishers, they all offered to give us the top spot – if we paid them. Now, I'm not a big fan of these "pay-to-play" tactics, but in this case, for a very low price, we could secure the #1 ranking on the top three sites that organically showed up at the top of Google when a person searched for "best software testing tools." And the total price? Just a few thousand dollars for a full year. I knew it wouldn't take many leads for us to show an ROI on that investment. So we paid the site publishers and we moved up to the #1 spot.

The impact was immediate. We saw a heavy increase in free trials through our website, and we could track them all back to these sites. Over the next six months, we generated over $1 million in pipeline directly sourced from that initial investment. I'd probably say I've never made a marketing investment before that had that type of ROI.

Before you just plow big money into campaigns, make sure you really know how to reach your buyer. How is your buyer getting the information to evaluate your solutions versus your competitors'? Dig into that customer journey and find all the potential touchpoints where you can reach and influence that buyer along the way. Those are the places where you can often make a big impact for a low marketing cost.

Always Be Testing

When I started in advertising in the '90s, research and testing took a long time and was very expensive. Doing advertising for P&G, we would first develop storyboards to test in focus groups. Then we would produce what's called an "animatic," which is an animated version of the commercial, and do a quantitative test. Once we had a winning ad, we would do the full production and then another quantitative and/or qualitative test of the ad before it would air on TV. It was an intense process for a 30-second ad. But it gave our clients the confidence that they were producing a TV ad that would generate positive results for their business.

Today, the game has changed. You can test and optimize on the fly. This gives marketers a powerful way to ensure they are getting the most out of their investments. Salespeople say, "Always Be Closing." Marketers today need to say, "Always Be Testing."

What's interesting is that many marketers are not doing much testing, or at least not doing as much as they should. One of the big lies you hear marketers say is: "We test everything." But, when you really dig in, you find out they really test nothing.

Why aren't more marketers actively testing their programs and campaigns? My guess is

there just isn't enough time. Marketers have so much coming at them today, it's hard to make testing a priority.

You also don't really know where to start with testing. What should you test? What knowledge will add value to your marketing results?

The answers to those questions will be very specific to your business. But I'll give you an example of the kind of testing that really improved performance at several companies I've worked with before.

A/B Testing

At PGi, we wanted to improve conversions on our website. We came up with a variety of hypotheses on what would improve our conversion rates. We talked about different headlines, button size and color, images, video, etc.

Using a tool called Optimizely, we tested these hypotheses. Optimizely is a great tool for quick A/B testing on your website. You don't need a team of developers involved. Once it's set up, a junior-level marketer can run tests all day long.

We had some really interesting findings from our tests. Changing the headlines and the style of buttons really didn't move the needle that much. What did move the needle surprised us.

We did a round of A/B testing where we tested one of our product pages with and without video thumbnails. These thumbnails are pretty small. When you click them, a modal window pops up that plays a larger version of the video.

In our A/B test, the version of the page with the video thumbnail had 65 conversions. The page without the video thumbnail? Only 11 conversions. That's almost a 500% increase in conversions on just that one single page!

What did we do with this information? You better believe we produced a lot more videos and added a lot more video thumbnails across our site! After we did that, we saw a significant increase in our conversions overall.

> You have to constantly come up with new hypotheses on what will improve your results.

My team actually meets about this every month. We brainstorm a list of the hypotheses we want to test out, then we select three to test. The rest go in a backlog for future testing. We spend the next four weeks doing the testing and then meet to review the results. It's a great process that keeps us thinking about ways to constantly get better.

Looking for things to test on your website? Here's are some ideas to get you started:

1. **Button size:** See what happens when you increase the size of the buttons.
2. **Button colors:** Play around with different colors and see what happens.
3. **Button messaging:** Try a variety of messaging to entice people to click: "click here," "get started," "free trial," "get a demo," "learn more." A small change in words can have a big impact on results.
4. **Video versus image:** Try adding a video to a page versus a static image.
5. **Offers:** Test a variety of offers to see what drives the most conversions.
6. **Page headlines:** Sometimes changing the key message of the page can improve your results.

Crowd Testing

Another great way to put your marketing to the test is through crowd testing. Sites like UserTesting.com provide a fast and low-cost way to get real feedback from real users.

We'll ask users to perform specific tasks like signing up for a free trial or downloading an ebook. Then you can actually see and hear the user as they are performing those tasks. This shows you how user-friendly your website is, but most importantly, it reveals any roadblocks that are preventing the user from completing the task.

In one instance, we realized that our website navigation was too confusing. The user couldn't find an important section of the site that had information on pricing. As a result, we completely overhauled the navigation to make it much easier. When we did the testing again, users were able to easily access the pricing page. This change led to a 100% increase in conversions on the site.

It's hard for me to advise you on what exactly you should be testing. All I can tell you is that testing provides a great opportunity for you and your marketing program to constantly get better. If you suck at marketing today, testing can help get you on the right track.

Creating Raving Fans

As a kid from New Jersey, I grew up a huge Bruce Springsteen fan. I remember seeing him for the first time in 1988 at the Philadelphia Spectrum during his Tunnel of Love tour.

It was probably one of the most transformative experiences of my life. I sat there as a 14-year-old kid, watching a man absolutely captivate an arena filled with 30,000 people. Looking around, it wasn't at all unusual to see grown men crying.

Since that first experience, I've seen Bruce in concert over 30 times. I even saw his Broadway show twice. The thing that always amazes me at a Springsteen show is the incredible connection he has with the audience. He gives everything at a performance, and the crowd truly appreciates every minute of it.

Usually I walk out of a Springsteen concert thinking, "Man, that was the best Bruce show I've ever seen." And that's pretty remarkable since I've seen him play so many times. He just seems to keep getting better.

Here's a great quote from Bruce: "Getting an audience is hard. Sustaining an audience is hard. It demands a consistency of thought, of purpose, and of action over a long period of time."

That really resonates with me as a marketer and underscores the commitment you must have to your customers. Whether you're selling to consumers or B2B clients, you have to work to ensure that your product or service is not just something they have to buy, but something they want to buy. Or even, something they love to buy.

We all have to realize that people hold companies to incredibly high standards. If you don't meet and exceed their expectations, they will go elsewhere. At the same time, research shows that companies are vastly underperforming. A study from American Express indicates that 95% of companies fail to exceed the expectations of their customers. 67% of customers say they would leave a business because of a bad experience. Yet only 1 in 26 customers actually complains.[5] This means the business will not even have the opportunity to fix the problem; they will just lose the customer.

When you also consider that acquiring a new customer is six to seven times more expensive than keeping an existing customer, it becomes clear that if you don't focus on customer experience, you will lose business.

Additionally, so few companies provide a great customer experience that if you do, you have the opportunity to really differentiate yourself from your competitors.

But it's not just about providing a good customer experience. It's about creating raving fans of your product

---

5. Afshar, Vala. "50 Important Customer Experience Stats for Business Leaders." *HuffPost*, 7 Dec. 2017, www.huffpost.com/entry/50-important-customer-exp_b_8295772.

or service. I always want my customers to feel about my company like I feel about Bruce Springsteen. Okay, maybe that's a stretch goal, but you have to aim high.

Let's explore two true stories of businesses working hard to create raving fans.

There was once a consultant who'd had a long week on the road and was flying back home. Before his plane took off, he sent a tweet to Mortons Steakhouse saying, "Hey @Mortons – can you meet me at the Newark airport with a porterhouse when I land in two hours? K, thanks ☺ "

And what happened next? A waiter from Morton's actually met him at the airport with a steak!

Elsewhere, there was a woman who frequently stayed at the Gaylord Opryland hotel in Nashville. She loved the Sharper Image noise machine in the room and wanted to buy one for herself, but she could not find it anywhere. On her next visit, the hotel left her one in her room as a gift. After receiving the noise machine, the woman said, "You reaffirmed that there are still companies out there focused on great service, and you've made a lifelong fan out of me."

I love these stories because they show how a business can create raving fans with just a bit of extra effort. Sometimes it's not even that hard. You just have to show you're listening and that you care.

One more story about creating raving fans

At ParkMobile, I spend a lot of time reading the app store reviews. It's a great way to learn what's working and what's not with our product. One day I came across a 1-star review. Here's what it said:

"I hate this app. Whatever happened to having a kiosk at the parking lot? I was on a date yesterday, and I believe it's rude to pull out your phone on a date. Instead of using my credit card at a kiosk like a normal establishment, I was forced to pull out my phone, create an account, and put in my license plate number and whatever other information it asked for. I'm surprised I didn't have to send them a picture of my social security card and a blood sample. All while my date waits for me to pay for the parking space. Waste of time. Then after that, I received 6 emails from ParkMobile over the course of the day, which I found most annoying. The date went well though! And the ParkMobile app will always be an inside joke between us."

Now, that's a great review! After I read it, I decided to reach out to the reviewer to see if we could make it right in some way. He was shocked that we contacted him. I guess people don't realize that companies actually read these reviews. I told him that we wanted to treat him and his date to another dinner, on us. We sent him a gift card so he could go back to the restaurant, and he said he appreciated it so much, he'd tell everyone about it.

I don't know how to measure the impact of what we did there. But it didn't take that much time or effort on our end, and we were able to turn a 1-star review into a big fan.

> There are opportunities every day to solve customer problems and make them feel special. Take the time to read the bad reviews, negative social posts, and customer complaints. Then do something about it.

For many, a great customer experience is just a dream. But, as Springsteen says in the song "Badlands," "Talk about a dream, try to make it real."

KEY TAKEAWAYS:

» Marketers need to focus on getting the basics right before moving on to more advanced tactics.

» Your customers are usually 70%–80% through the buying process before they engage with a sales rep. Marketers need to focus on what customers are doing during that evaluation time.

» Search engines and your website are key to attracting customers to your product. They're your virtual sales rep.

» As a marketer, you can do anything, but you can't do everything. You need to focus on fewer things that will make the biggest impact on the business.

» Modern marketers have to be flexible. They are quick to change course if something doesn't work.

» When starting a new job, don't take on too much too soon. It's good to have a quick win strategy to build credibility within the organization.

» Core values create an important foundation for the company. You can't build a strong brand if you don't understand what your company's values are. Once you define the core values, you have to work hard to make sure employees understand and live those values every day.

» Pay close attention to your brand personality. Is it going to win customers over or turn them off?

» A tagline should describe the true soul of the brand in just a few words.

» The key to reaching your buyer is to find the "watering holes" where buyers go to learn about the products in your category.

» Testing is critical to improving marketing performance. A/B testing and crowd testing provide opportunities to optimize your marketing program and improve results.

» The best brands work to solve customer problems and make customers feel special. The goal is to turn customers into raving fans.

PART 3:
HAVING A CAREER
THAT DOESN'T SUCK

Career Basics

Your Personal Brand

When I was a mid-level manager, I desperately wanted to break through to the next level. I wanted that VP title. But I was struggling to move up in the company. I had been there five years, and I didn't see a path for me. I would ask my boss about it, and he couldn't give me a straight answer. "Just keep doing what you're doing, Jeff," he would say. "Things will eventually work out for you."

"Eventually" – that's not the word I was looking for, especially after five years of doing really good work and getting stellar performance reviews. The company clearly valued me as an employee. They kept putting me in different leadership programs and even provided me with my own professional coach.

At some point it became evident that I was not going to move up unless someone left the company. And there was a big layer of people ahead of me. I just didn't see a path forward. If you aren't going to move up, your other option is to move out. And that's what I decided to do.

This is a decision people make every day. The average person changes jobs about 12 times during their career.[6] Millennials actually change jobs four times by the age of 32.[7]

---

6. Doyle, Alison. "How Often Do People Change Jobs?" *The Balance Careers*, 15 June 2020, www.thebalancecareers.com/how-often-do-people-change-jobs-2060467.

7. Long, Heather. "The New Normal: 4 Job Changes by the Time You're 32." *CNNMoney*, 12 Apr. 2016, money.cnn.com/2016/04/12/news/economy/millennials-change-jobs-frequently/index.html.

And the #1 reason why people change jobs so frequently is lack of opportunity.[8]

The truth is frequent job change is the new normal for most people today. Because of that, professionals have to develop a new skill – building and maintaining a strong personal brand.

When I decided I wanted to make a career move, I really didn't have any kind of personal brand outside the company. This became painfully evident as I started sending my resume around.

You see, my title at the time was "Senior Marketing Manager." I'd argue that given the responsibilities of my job, I would probably have been a Director or VP in most companies. I managed a 15-person team and a multi-million-dollar marketing budget. I had an important portfolio of projects that had very high visibility in the company. I reported directly to the CMO and had a lot of facetime with the CEO and other C-level executives. I felt like I was a senior-level member of the team, and I was paid pretty well. In fact, my salary was much closer to a VP level than a manager salary.

Having the "manager" title probably wouldn't have been a problem if I'd wanted to stay at the company forever. But when I decided to make a move, it became highly problematic. I had been off the job market for five years, so I really didn't know where to start. I sent my resume around to some recruiters I knew, and I started applying for positions I found online. I didn't get much response.

Finally, one recruiter returned my call. He had a marketing manager position open that he thought could be a good fit. Marketing Manager? I was looking for a VP role.

The recruiter said, "Well Jeff, you know you don't really have the title. So, I can't put you up for VP jobs."

---

8. Tegze, Jan. "The 7 Reasons Why People Change Jobs." *Sourcing and Recruiting News*, 6 Apr. 2021, recruitingdaily. com/7-big-reasons-people-change-jobs.

That was a tough pill to swallow. I was being told I couldn't get a VP job because I didn't have a VP title. So what could I do? I told the recruiter I'd be interested in learning about the manager job. Maybe I'd do a lateral move and hope there would be more opportunity to move up to that VP level quicker at another company.

"Okay, let's submit your resume," said the recruiter. "Just tell me your salary requirements."

When I told him what I was making at my company, there was a long silence.

"Oh, that's way too high for this job," the recruiter said. "Would you consider a bit of a pay cut for this opportunity?"

A pay cut? Seriously? I had just busted my ass for five years, building the marketing team and driving measurable results that generated revenue for my company, and now this recruiter was telling me that I couldn't be a VP and I would have to take a pay cut.

I realized I was in a classic Catch-22 situation. I couldn't get the VP job because I didn't have the VP title. I couldn't get a manager job because I made too much money.

This realization was crushing.

I knew I needed to do something, but I didn't know what to do. I felt helpless. This was definitely one of the low points of my career.

After talking to the recruiter, I needed to clear my head. I turned on the TV and watched some Seinfeld. In the episode, George Costanza was depressed because he felt like such a loser. He's sitting with Jerry and Elaine at the diner. Elaine tells George that an attractive woman is looking at him from across the room and encourages him to go talk to her.

George says, "Elaine, bald men with no jobs and no money who live with their parents don't approach strange women."

Jerry then encourages George to do the opposite. He says, "If every instinct you have is wrong, then the opposite would have to be right."

George walks up to the woman and says, "My name is George, I'm unemployed, and I live with my parents." The woman ends up going on a date with George.

This scene got me thinking about my job search. I realized that what I was doing was not working. I wasn't defining myself.

As they say, if you don't define yourself, someone else will. That's what was happening. I was letting recruiters and hiring managers define me by my title.

Maybe I needed to do the opposite. I needed to reshape my brand. I needed to position myself as an executive marketer. But how do you do this? I mean, you can't just print out a t-shirt that says "I'm a CMO" and expect people to believe it.

My first step was to think about this question: what do companies want in an executive marketer?

I spent an afternoon going through CMO and VP of Marketing job descriptions I found online. After reading about 100 different postings, I boiled it down to five key things:

1. Vision for the brand
2. Ability to lead a team
3. Understanding of current marketing trends
4. Ability to measure and drive results
5. Skills to communicate the message

I looked at the list and thought, "Wow, this is me." The fact is, I had tons of work examples I could talk about for each of these points. But how would I get this message out?

> Well-crafted bullet points on a resume would not be enough. I needed to find forums where I could show what I could do.

5 KEY ELEMENTS
of your EXECUTIVE BRAND

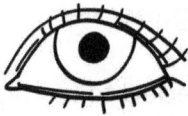

VISION:
For a clear picture of your abilities + future goals.

LEADERSHIP:
To guide both a team and an audience.

UNDERSTANDING:
Of your objectives, strengths, limitations, and subject matter.

MEASUREMENT:
The capacity to accurately, quantitatively, + qualitatively assess your work.

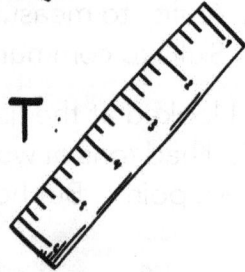

COMMUNICATION:
The ability to convey your ideas and values clearly to others.

I had always been a pretty good public speaker, and I enjoyed presenting in front of an audience, so I thought maybe I should try to speak at some marketing events. That might be a good start.

I googled Atlanta marketing events and found an upcoming panel discussion hosted by B2B Magazine. They didn't list any speakers on the website, so I emailed the event organizer and asked who would be on the panel. The organizer said they were still in the process of filling the spots. I told her I'd be interested in participating, and she immediately signed me up.

I thought I did pretty well on the panel, and there were about 100 people who showed up. After the event the moderator, who was an editor for B2B Magazine, asked if I would be interested in contributing a monthly article to the magazine. I told him yes, I'd be honored.

Suddenly, I was speaking at events and writing for a national publication. I spent time researching other marketing events in the area where I could potentially speak. I learned that most events have a "call for speakers" link on their website. I got pretty good at filling out these applications and getting accepted to speak. Next thing I knew, I was on the "speaking circuit" for Atlanta marketing events. After I spoke at one event, I would get asked to speak at another, then another.

I also launched my own blog[9] and wrote one post a week for an entire year.

The process of writing and creating presentations really helped me sharpen my thinking about key marketing topics, a skill that would serve me very well as I interviewed for jobs. If a hiring manager asked me what I thought about social media or brand strategy, I would be able to deliver a concise and compelling answer because I had recently written about those topics. I wasn't just thinking about them for the first time when asked the question in an interview.

---

9. Check out my blog at: singlemindedproposition.com.

I even took my show on the road. The company I worked for had a large sales team across the country, so I'd try to schedule trips to visit the teams in key markets that coincided with events seeking speakers. I remember one marketing conference in Dallas where I made a pretty big splash. The Eagles and Cowboys had a big game coming up that weekend with playoff implications.

As an Eagles fan, I was in the lion's den. There were about 500 people in the room. The Eagles and Cowboys have a legendary rivalry – we don't like each other at all. Now, I could have not mentioned being an Eagles fan, but what fun would that be? Instead, I started my presentation showing pictures from the game when the Eagles had beat the Cowboys earlier that season.

I immediately got booed. But it was all in good fun and really created a lot of engagement with my presentation. I think the audience actually appreciated it; when I finished the talk, I got a very nice round of applause. I guess even the Cowboys fans appreciated the strong content.

After I got off stage, the MC said, "Ladies and gentlemen, please welcome to the stage the VP of Marketing for the Dallas Cowboys." I didn't realize someone from the Cowboys was going on after me. Awkward!

The Cowboys marketing guy got up on stage and made a bad joke about Eagles fans. He got a few sympathy laughs, but that was it. As he presented, I checked Twitter and saw that I had several hundred notifications. Uh oh, I thought. What did I do?

I started scrolling through and saw I was getting a ton of Twitter hate from early on in my presentation.

"Who does this guy think he is?"

"This guy is going to get booed off the stage."

"Why would they invite an Eagles fan to present at this conference?"

Then, suddenly the sentiment in the tweets started to shift.

"Eagles fan is dropping some serious knowledge."

"Once I got past the Eagles stuff, this session is really good."

"Eagles fan just delivered best presentation of the conference."

And my personal favorite:

"This Cowboys marketing guy is pretty boring. Can they bring back that Eagles fan?"

It was fun reading and responding to all the tweets. One person posted a screenshot of top-trending topics in Dallas during the hour I was presenting. For that short time, I was #1 trending on Twitter, even above Ellen DeGeneres!

Optimizing Your LinkedIn Presence

As my personal brand grew, I needed to make sure I was reinforcing that brand at all the key touchpoints. I realized that LinkedIn was becoming increasingly important as a professional platform. As I analyzed my LinkedIn profile, I saw that it was just an online version of my resume. I wasn't really leveraging all the features of the LinkedIn platform to showcase my personal brand.

I did a complete overhaul of my LinkedIn profile, using it to tell the story of my career journey, rather than just the usual resume bullet points. I added a lot of multimedia assets to my profile to really showcase my work, and I made sure my LinkedIn headline truly reflected my brand. I see so many people on LinkedIn who use their current job title as their headline. That doesn't really tell a prospective employer much about you.

So rather than "Marketing Manager," I updated my profile to say "Experienced Marketing Leader and All-Around Nice Guy." Once I made that change, I was surprised how many recruiters started checking me out on LinkedIn. There's a big difference in perception between a "marketing manager" and a "marketing leader."

And why add "All-Around Nice Guy"? Well first, I think am a pretty nice guy. Second, it grabs attention. Not many people post personal attributes in their headline. I found that having "nice guy" helped me break through the clutter of all the other marketers out there. I'd frequently get emails from recruiters saying, "Since you're an 'all-around nice guy,' I thought I'd reach out." That saying is still on my LinkedIn profile today.

I want any prospective employer to be able to look at my LinkedIn profile and really get to know me. I want them to be able to look at work I've done and things I've written so they can get a full picture of exactly what I can bring to their company. That's why it's critical to make sure your LinkedIn profile accurately reflects the brand you're building.

> If your LinkedIn profile looks like your resume, you're doing it wrong.

The Results

After about a year of consistent focus on my personal brand, things really started to happen for me. I learned that when you put yourself out there, people gravitate to you. I met so many great people at conferences that I've kept in touch with, and I exponentially grew my connections on LinkedIn. My network was getting really strong.

As marketing jobs came up, people in my network would constantly refer me to the recruiter or hiring manager. I was starting to get considered for the kinds of opportunities I wanted. I was getting calls for the VP of Marketing gigs.

I remember one recruiter calling me and saying, "I've had five different people tell me I should talk to you about this job. Everybody seems to know you." That's the impact of having a strong network.

I ended up going through the interview process for two different VP jobs. I got offers for both positions. Looking back, it's kind of amazing to think about. Just a year before, I'd felt like I was stuck in mid-level management forever. Now I had two companies bidding against each other to bring me on board.

None of this would have been possible if I hadn't "done the opposite." So, big thanks to George Costanza for the career inspiration.

Anatomy of a Good LinkedIn Profile

How do you build a strong LinkedIn profile? Well, it's really not that difficult. You probably already have most of the important content documented in your resume. You just have to spend some time making it work for LinkedIn. Here's what you need:

A good profile picture

You want to make sure you have a really good professional headshot for LinkedIn. It's not just another social media platform where you post a random picture with your pet, kids, or significant other. This is a picture of just you. It should be a headshot, not full body. Make sure it's somewhat recent (taken in the last five years) and that it reflects what you want to convey about your personal brand. If you are more of a formal person, wear a suit and tie in the picture. If you're more casual, wear a blazer over a t-shirt. Just make sure the quality of the photo is good.

A strong headline

This is what a lot of people get wrong in their LinkedIn profile. People just post their job title and company as their "headline." That's not what the headline is for. The headline is your personal value proposition. Make sure it fully communicates your personal brand. It's a good opportunity to highlight special skills, experiences, accolades, accomplishments, or just something unique about you. It's also important for LinkedIn's search algorithm, so make sure you have the right keywords to attract potential recruiters. You only have 111 characters, so you need to make them count.

A few good examples:

» Jo Ann Herold: Chief Marketing Officer @ The Honey Baked Ham Co * Proven Brand & Transformation Leader With Rapid Growth Track Record * B2C & B2B * Purpose Zealot * Board Member
» Kira Mondrus: CMO | Global Marketing | Strategy | Demand Generation | Brand Building | Customer Retention | Go-to-Market
» Jennifer Davis: Chief Marketing Officer (CMO), Learfield IMG College | Former Amazon Web Services | Author (Well Made Decisions, publication August 2021)
» Jacqui Chew: Creative Problem-solver / Coalition-builder / Storyteller / TEDx Licensee / CMO
» Jessica Garrett: VP Marketing @ Alpha Comm | Brand builder | Speaker | Revenue creator | Food lover
» Angela Culver: Group Vice President, Marketing & Measurement @Oracle | Customer-Obsessed | Advisor | Data-Driven | Branding | Marketing Operations

Tell your story

The "About" section gives you the chance to tell your story. Don't just put something generic or a boilerplate bio. Really take advantage of the opportunity to communicate who you are and what you are all about. Give the reader the chance to really get to know you. I recommend writing it in the first person, just like you would tell your story in a job interview. Also, don't be afraid to throw a few personal items in – how many kids you have, hobbies, pets, etc.

Showcase your content

The next section on a LinkedIn profile is called "Featured." This is where you can post work samples, such as a video of you presenting at a conference, an article you wrote or were quoted in, podcast interviews, or samples of projects you have worked on. It's basically your online portfolio. Fill it with the best stuff you have. You should also add additional content under each job in the experience section.

Tell why you made job changes

One thing hiring mangers and recruiters always wonder is why a candidate has moved from job to job. In the "Experience" section on LinkedIn, you have the opportunity to explain why. Again, this section should not just be bullets from your resume. Tell the story of your career progression through each position. Maybe you left one job to do something more entrepreneurial or got an opportunity to move into a more senior level. You can also explain any gaps in your experience if you took time off to go back to graduate school, have kids, etc. Really use the text in the "Experience" section to go deeper than you did in the "About" section.

Get recommendations

When I'm interviewing job candidates, I always read the LinkedIn recommendations. It's a great way to do a quick reference check. But don't just go for quantity – it's the quality of the recommendations that really matters. Try to get more senior-level people to write them. Ideally, these should be people you've worked directly for, and it's generally a good practice to have a recommendation for each job that you've had. If you are at an executive level, it's also good to have recommendations from your direct reports or peers.

List your accomplishments

LinkedIn gives you real estate at the bottom of your profile to list out your "Accomplishments." These could be awards, published articles, patents, organizations, languages, and more. It's not the most important section of a LinkedIn profile, but it does give you a chance to showcase a lot of things that make you unique.

> If you focus on the seven points listed above, you'll have a LinkedIn profile that builds your personal brand and helps you stand out from the crowd.

Nurture Yourself

Fitness has a big impact on mental acuity and is a good hedge against the stress that goes along with a career in marketing.

A few years back, I was at a conference, and an executive recruiter for Spencer Stuart did a presentation about what companies are looking for in executive-level marketers. He made the point that the demands on executives today are very intense. To be effective in the role, you have to have the skills and experience necessary, but you also have to be both mentally and physically fit. This was probably the first time I had heard anyone link physical fitness and career success.

For many years, I've been into fitness. I try to work out as much as I can, usually at least five days a week. But it hasn't always been that way.

When I was in high school, I played basketball every day. I was really skinny. I could eat whatever I wanted, and I definitely did not have a healthy diet. Plus, I had a huge appetite. There were never leftovers at my house.

But as I got older, I played less basketball and still ate the same quantity of food. The result was that I gained weight. To hide the extra pounds, I just started buying oversized pants and baggy shirts.

When my wife was pregnant with our first child, I started to gain what they call "sympathy weight," meaning that I would eat more to match my wife's pregnancy weight gain with some pounds of my own. Then my wife had the baby, and the weight just melted off her. For me, it wasn't so easy.

So I decided to do something drastic to lose weight: I signed up for one of those outdoor boot camps in the local park. It was a full month of dieting and working out at 6:00am every day, which was pretty early for me, but I thought I could handle it since it was only for a few weeks.

After a month of boot camp, I dropped ten pounds and felt great, so I decided to do a second month. Then I did a third and fourth month. At this point, I was used to getting up at 5:30 am, so I just kept doing it. I was so into it that I actually became a boot camp instructor for about four years.

In 2012, I "retired" from boot camp and switched to spin class. Every morning I'd wake up early and go to the gym to get on the bike. It was really hard, and sometimes I felt like I was going to die, but I always left feeling super-energized. It's really a great way to start the day. More recently, I bought a Peloton bike, so now I do competitive spin classes from the comfort of my home. (If you want to race me, my leaderboard name is "BaldGuy." Fair warning, I put up pretty high numbers, so don't come at me unless you bring your A-game!)

Obviously, there are lots of physical benefits to working out. But what I've found is that exercise has actually made me a better marketer.

Better productivity

I used to be one of those people who walked into the office like a zombie. I couldn't even talk to anyone until I had two cups of coffee. It just took me a while to get into the flow of the day. But since I've been exercising every morning, I come into the office wide awake and ready to go. I get a fast start; I get more done. On days that I don't exercise, I just don't feel as good, and I find myself getting tired in the late afternoon. I'd estimate that exercise gives me an extra hour of productivity each day. Over the year, that can add up to 260 hours or about 11 days.

Stress management

There have been a lot of studies about how exercise relieves stress. According to the Mayo Clinic, exercise pumps up your endorphins, which are the brain's "feel-good neurotransmitters."[10] I'm a believer. A few years ago, during a particularly stressful time at work, daily exercise helped me keep it together. If I didn't work out on a given day, I would get home at night so exhausted by the stress that I'd have to go right to bed. It was an awful feeling. So during stressful times, I always make sure to get a workout in. It just keeps me sane.

Improving creativity

At its core, marketing is about new ideas that drive better results. But coming up with new ideas isn't always easy. I've found that some of my best ideas come to me when I'm exercising. I'm not sure what it is about exercise that gets the creative juices flowing, but sometimes I get back from a long run with tons of new ideas. The challenge is remembering them and writing them down as soon as I get home. According to an article in *Newsweek*, "Almost every dimension of cognition improves from 30 minutes of aerobic exercise, and creativity is no exception. The type of exercise doesn't matter, and the boost lasts for at least two hours afterward."[11] So if you're looking for a creative solution to a business problem, go for a jog and it might come to you.

Higher energy levels

When you work in marketing, you have to be high energy. You have to sell your ideas and your vision. But if you

10. "Exercise and Stress: Get Moving to Manage Stress." *Mayo Clinic*, 18 Aug. 2020, www.mayoclinic.org/healthy-lifestyle/stress-management/in-depth/exercise-and-stress/art-20044469

11. Bronson, Po, and Ashley Merryman. "Forget Brainstorming." *Newsweek*, 23 Jan. 2014, www.newsweek.com/forget-brainstorming-74223.

have low energy, that's hard to do. I find that exercise gives me an extra boost of energy that lasts throughout the day. If I have a big presentation, I always have to get a workout in that morning. It's the energy from the exercise that makes me a better presenter.

Competitive edge

I usually work out in competitive group activities. In a spin class, you compete with other riders to see who can get the most points. It's a lot of fun, but I have to admit that when I get the highest score in a class, it feels great. I find that the competitive drive carries over to my work. As Vince Lombardi said, "Winning is not a sometime thing; it's an all-time thing. You don't win once in a while, you don't do things right once in a while, you do them right all the time. Winning is habit." That's a good insight. Doing highly competitive workouts has made me more driven to try harder at work and deliver better results for my company.

I firmly believe that exercise has done a lot for me in my career. I encourage anyone – regardless of your level in the company, your age, your current fitness level – to take the time every week to take care of your body.

> Don't sacrifice your physical fitness for your career when it can actually help improve it.

Finding a Job that Doesn't Suck

Here's a tough question to ask yourself: Are you the right "fit" for your company?

If the answer is yes, my guess is that you're probably pretty happy at your job. But if the answer is "not sure" or "no," you're probably very unhappy, even if you work for a great company.

Several years back, I was working at what many would consider to be a great company. The business was growing rapidly, and the company took really good care of its employees. The only problem was that the culture was just not quite right for me, and there were a lot of unwritten rules about how you were expected to behave in the workplace.

Here are a few examples:

- » Never question or debate someone senior to you, even if you do it in a polite and productive way.
- » Always hide your emotions. Never get angry, even if it's completely justified.
- » If you're in a meeting with company executives, always let your boss do all the talking.
- » If you're giving a presentation, it should not be fun or entertaining in any way because that distracts from the content.

Anyone who didn't follow the "rules" would be identified as a "problem," and unfortunately, I got pegged as one of those "problem" people.

Here are some things you should know about me: I'm a passionate guy. I love talking about business and debating strategy. I want to figure out how to solve tough problems and move the company forward. When I worked in a mid-level position, I was never afraid to share my thoughts and ideas with senior executives. I'd sometimes show my emotions when I got frustrated. That's just how I'm wired.

In many companies, those would be good traits for an employee. But at this particular company, the way I was behaving was holding me back. When I would get a performance review, the common theme was that my work was excellent, but I didn't follow the "rules."

There was a phrase that would often come up in my reviews: "lacks self-awareness."

Honestly, that kind of feedback would drive me nuts. The one thing I did not lack was self-awareness. I was completely aware of my behavior. And I was aware that it would sometimes make my co-workers or boss uncomfortable. I was always focused on doing good work that would help move the business, and I was delivering results that no one could argue with.

But I started to realize that my behavior was limiting my career at this company. Just doing good work wasn't enough to get me to the next level. I had to start behaving differently.

I decided to make a change. I started to really "dial it back." I wouldn't debate. I'd keep quiet in meetings, only speaking if spoken to. I never let my frustrations show, and I tried my best to play nice with everyone.

It wasn't easy. I wasn't used to being the quiet one in meetings. I wasn't used to holding back when I felt like I could solve a problem or contribute to a conversation.

But as I changed my behavior, things started happening for me in the company. My boss was happier with me. I got great feedback from peers in my 360 reviews. I even got a promotion!

But it was killing me on the inside. I just felt like I wasn't myself anymore, and I would come home from work every day absolutely exhausted. It's hard work trying to be someone you're not.

During this time, I also felt like my work really suffered. I wasn't bringing the same energy to my projects. It felt like I was just going through the motions, but that didn't seem to matter because people had started to see me as a "company guy" with a bright future.

Then it happened. I had a relapse. I was giving a presentation in front of the marketing department, and I started off by showing a slide with a picture of my kids. I made a joke about how my daughter has an amazing head of hair while her daddy is completely bald. I said people would always joke to me, "Well, she didn't get her hair from you, Jeff!" Then I'd say, "Well, the joke is on them," and show a picture of myself as a kid with a thick head of hair like my daughter's. I got a huge laugh. It was a nice way to break the ice and build rapport with the audience. But I knowingly did violate the "no entertaining presentations" rule.

After the presentation, I was called into the boss' office and told not to put pictures of my kids in my presentations again. He told me that it distracted from the content of the presentation, and it wasn't funny.

There were so many things I wanted to say to him. It was one slide in a 45-minute presentation. And it definitely was funny. Those weren't sympathy laughs I was getting. People were genuinely cracking up. But I didn't argue. I just apologized and left his office.

I went back to my desk completely deflated. That day I came to the difficult realization that this was not the right company for me. I just wasn't a good fit. It was time for me to leave.

I polished up my resume and started a job search. A few months later, I resigned. When I walked out the door on my last day, I felt like a weight was lifted from my shoulders.

The new company I joined ended up being a much better fit. I could really be myself at work, and I would show up every day excited to be there. Everything about my style that had worked against me at the last company worked in my favor at this new company. And showing pictures of your kids in presentations was not only accepted but also encouraged.

I have a feeling that many people can relate to this story. I'm sure some of you are struggling with this exact issue right now.

All I can tell you is that it's not enough just to work for a great company. You have to work for a company that's the right fit for you – a place where you don't have to change who you are in order to be successful.

You only get one career. Why spend it unhappy?

Building a Flexible and Focused Career

Interviewing for a Marketing Job

One of the most common questions I get from younger marketing professionals is, "What do I need to do or say in a job interview?" Here are a few ways I've seen successful candidates stand out from the rest and get the gig.

Be Prepared

Know the company

As a candidate, I don't expect you to have an in-depth understanding of the company or industry, but you'd better have some basic information when you do the interview. Spend time looking at the company's website, reading recent news articles, and looking at social media posts. If it's a public company, make sure to read the most recent earnings report. You should expect to get some questions related to what's going on at the company, so be prepared.

Understand who you are interviewing with

Before you go on an interview, make sure to ask the recruiter the names of all the people you'll be meeting with. Do some LinkedIn research to understand who they are and what they do. This shows that you took the time to do your homework. You may also find some interesting nuggets you can bring up during the interview to build rapport. Maybe you went to the same college, or you have friends in common. And never go into an interview and ask the person across the table from you, "What do you do for the company?" I actually had a candidate say this to me once. He seemed shocked when I said, "I'm the CMO." Not a good look.

A compelling reason you are interested in the job

I'm always surprised when I ask people why they want to work at the company, and they give me a blank stare, then fumble through some generic talking points. This happens more often than you would think. Do yourself a favor: before going to an interview, write down specifically why you want the job. Be as specific as possible. If you can't come up with a reason, maybe you shouldn't be interviewing for that job.

Engage with the interviewer

Enthusiasm

This is one of the first things I look for in a candidate. How enthusiastic are they about marketing and the company? I generally like to hire "marketing geeks," meaning that they love to "geek out" on all things marketing. I really love when candidates get excited about a campaign they're working on or a new technology they're using. This shows the energy they bring to the job, and often that energy can be infectious.

Thoughts on marketing and your experience

You're interviewing for a marketing job, so you'd better be prepared to talk marketing. Be ready with multiple examples of campaigns or programs you've worked on. Talk about lessons you've learned in your career from successes and failures, and share some thoughts on how you would approach marketing for the company. I often ask candidates what they think of our current marketing program and what they might do differently. I love it when I get specific examples. Don't be afraid to put together a 1-pager or even a short PowerPoint deck with your ideas. It will make you stand out from the other candidates.

Commitment to marketing and personal development

I always like seeing marketers who continually seek to learn and grow in their craft. Completing certifications is a great way to keep up with the latest technologies and expand your expertise. And if the company has a martech solution that you have a certification for, that really positions you well for the job. Also, involvement or leadership roles in the local marketing community show your passion for marketing. These communities are great ways to learn from peers and grow your network.

Ask good questions

It seems obvious, but I'm constantly shocked when I ask the candidate if they have any questions, and they say, "no." That happens more than you would think. Are you kidding me? You have no questions about the role or the company? For me, that's an automatic disqualifier for the candidate. Here's a tip: write down ten questions. Ask as many as you can before the interview ends. Here are a few general questions that are good to ask in any interview:

- » What is the culture like here?
- » What KPIs will be important for this role?
- » How will you determine success for this role?
- » What are some of the biggest challenges for this role?
- » What is your management style like?
- » Can you tell me about the expectations for the first 30-60-90 days?
- » What are the characteristics of employees who are successful here?
- » Will there be professional development opportunities?
- » How does the marketing team interact with other parts of the company?
- » What makes you most excited about the company?

And in case you ever find yourself interviewing with me in the future, here are two questions that I will probably ask you. Come prepared!

- » What's your proudest accomplishment in your career?
- » What's the biggest disappointment or failure you've had in your career?

After the interview

Send a thank-you email

Okay, this is a personal pet peeve of mine. So many candidates do not send thank-you notes. I just don't get it. Take five minutes and send an email to thank the person for meeting with you. It's not that hard. And it allows you to reinforce (1) why you are a strong candidate, (2) why you want the job, and (3) that you appreciate being considered for the opportunity. If I don't get a thank-you note from a candidate, that's another disqualifier. You don't need to send a handwritten note because it would take too long to get delivered. You need that thank-you email to go out within 12 hours, while the interview is still fresh in the mind of the person you interviewed with.

Making an Impact

After my freshman year in college at American University, I had the opportunity to intern for the mayor of Cherry Hill, Susan Bass Levin. Since I was studying political science, I thought it would be a great way to learn how government works.

It was a great experience. I spent most of my days answering constituent letters and phone calls. One of the main complaints was about the condition of the medians on Route 70, the main state road that ran through the town. The medians had overgrown weeds that were about six feet high. It was not a good look for the main transportation artery of the city.

Since it was a state road, it wasn't the city's responsibility to landscape it. But it had become a total eyesore and was creating a lot of angst for city leadership. Attempts to get the state government to cut the weeds had failed.

The city didn't have the budget to pay for a major landscaping project along this large stretch of highway, so we decided to organize an Adopt-a-Highway program, getting local businesses along Route 70 to help fund the project. My job was to solicit the businesses for donations. I spent my days going door to door, asking for contributions.

The businesses I talked to were all very excited about the program and more than happy to donate. They had long been frustrated by the condition of the median strip in front of their businesses. As one owner said to me, "I try to keep my store so nice, then I look across the street and see six-foot-high weeds."

After a month, we had raised more than enough money to hire a landscaper to clear the weeds and plant some nice flowers and shrubbery along the section of Route 70 that ran through Cherry Hill. Even today, when I go home to visit, I enjoy driving on the road and seeing that the landscaping still exists.

For my efforts to coordinate the Adopt-a-Highway program, Mayor Levin named a day after me in Cherry Hill. In case you're interested, August 8, 1993, is officially "Jeff Perkins Day." Pretty cool, huh? Not many people can say they have a day named after them in their hometown.

The thing I really liked about working for the mayor and doing that project was it gave me the opportunity to make an impact I could see. There's a very clear "before" and "after." Early on in my career, this was a good lesson on what gets me excited to go to work every day. I want to be able to make a difference. I want to do work that moves the needle in some way.

Even today, I'm drawn to the opportunities where I can make a tangible difference. Whether it's rebuilding a department or helping get a startup off the ground, I need to see the direct impact on the business.

I would never take a job that was all about navigating a bureaucracy or just checking boxes on a to-do list. Give me the hard jobs, the ones that require tough decisions. The ones where you have to roll up your sleeves and get dirty. The ones where you can't hide and you're putting yourself out there to be judged by the world. Because those are the jobs where you have the opportunity to make the biggest impact.

I encourage anyone reading this to think about your job. What makes you most excited at work? Where do you get the greatest satisfaction? As you navigate through your career, find those opportunities where the job aligns with the things that make you happy at work.

When to Leave a Job

When is the right time to leave a job?

That's a tough question. You don't want to make a move too early and miss out on the growth and financial benefits of your current job. You also don't want to wait until it's too late and you're pushed out, then find yourself desperately trying to find your next gig. Figuring out the "right time" requires a lot of thought.

I've had a lot of jobs in my career. It's probably an occupational hazard of being a marketer. We generally don't stick around that long for one reason or another that I've discussed in other chapters of this book.

If you are thinking about when to make a move, here are some things to consider.

Do you actually like your job?

I know it's a simple question, but you have to be honest with yourself. Do you have fun when you go to work every day? Do you like the job you're doing? Do you enjoy the industry you work in? If the answer to the majority of these questions is "no," you might be ready for a change. I see a lot of people who are unhappy at work, and that's a horrible feeling – I've been there. It's exhausting to slog through a day at a place you don't want to be, doing work you're not excited about. So if you don't like your job, it might be time to explore some other options out there.

Do you like the people you work with?

We spend the majority of our week with our co-workers, much more time than we spend with friends and family. If you don't like the people you're working with, that company just may not be for you. When you really like your boss and your team, it makes going to work every day a pleasure. You don't have to be best friends with your co-workers, but at least you should enjoy being around each other. I've found that the highest-performing teams don't just *have* to work together; they actually *like* to work together.

Is there growth opportunity?

At some point, you will hit the ceiling in your job. You might want to get promoted, but there's no place for you to go in your current organization. This is a tough spot because you might like your job, but you also want to continue to advance your career. That has happened to me a few times, and I've had to make the difficult decision to move out to move up.

Is the company doing well?

There will be times when you're professionally doing well, but the business just isn't. The reality for marketers is that if the company is struggling and not hitting its numbers, one of the first things to go is usually marketing. In some cases, you just have to read the tea leaves. If the business is in decline, you will want to make sure you keep your options open.

Are you paid fairly?

When you work in a company for an extended period, you will probably be a bit underpaid compared to people who have joined more recently. If you are at the company for five years, getting modest merit increases annually, your base salary just won't increase that much over time. You want to make sure you understand what people like you are making in the local market for similar roles. There are plenty of websites out there that share this information, and recruiters can also give you a range. If you feel like you're significantly underpaid and can make a lot more elsewhere, it may be worth looking at those opportunities.

How good is the job market?

This is a critical factor when considering a move. If it's a tight job market, you may want to delay your search and wait for a better time when there will be more opportunities. The last thing you want when making a career move is to just settle for something. It's a good practice to keep in touch with the key marketing recruiters in the area to gauge how hot or cold the market is before you put yourself out there.

Are you leaving money on the table?

Timing is everything when making a career change. You want to make sure you're not making a foolish financial move. Before you accept any offer, you have to know when your annual bonus will pay out, your 401k match will vest, and any other financial incentives out there. The key is to make sure you're maximizing your financial position in any career move. At times, the new opportunity may be so attractive that you're willing to walk away from some money at your current job. Just make sure you understand what that money is. In some cases, you can negotiate a signing bonus from your new employer to incentivize you to start before the annual bonus from your current job pays out.

What's your personal stock worth?

I'm not talking about stock you might own in the business. Think of yourself as "stock." There will be times when your stock is up and times when your stock is down. The key is to make a move when your personal stock value is high. For example, when I was CMO at QASymphony, we'd just raised a $40 million Series C from Insight Venture Partners. That's a pretty big event for a startup company. As the CMO, I had a lot of positive exposure; at that time, my stock value was very high. That's when I decided to make my move, and I had plenty of great opportunities come my way.

Leaving a job always has to be a very careful decision. Before making any moves, ask yourself the eight questions above and consult with your peers and mentors to get their advice. Make sure when you sign that offer letter, you feel confident that you are absolutely making the right choice.

The Low Point: What Happens When Your Career Hits Rock Bottom and How to Turn It Around

In your career, you will have highs and lows. My all-time low came in 2003. I had just graduated from Emory's Goizueta Business School with my MBA, but that didn't translate into a great job at graduation.

I came out of school into a tough job market that was recovering after the "dotcom" bust. The traditional MBA-type companies were no longer doing "strategic hiring," and a high percentage of my classmates graduated without jobs.

Going to a top business school in Atlanta, I thought I might be able to score a position at one of the big companies in town – Coke, Home Depot, Delta, Georgia Pacific, etc. No luck. Emory's business school is actually named after former Coke CEO Roberto Goizueta, but that didn't seem to help me or my classmates get a job there.

We had to get creative with our job searches. We had to look beyond the traditional MBA jobs. I ended up getting a job with a startup that made floor mats with college football logos. Not your typical post-MBA job, but I felt lucky to be getting a paycheck. Many of my classmates were graduating with nothing.

It's a good lesson for people considering going back to school for an MBA. There is no guarantee that you'll get the job you want after graduation. Actually, there's no guarantee you'll get any job after graduation. That doesn't mean you shouldn't go back to school. You just have to go in with your eyes wide open and recognize the risks.

After a few months working at this startup selling floor mats, I realized that it wasn't the job for me. I really wanted to go back up to New York, where I'd lived before business school. I knew I couldn't realistically interview for jobs in NY while working in Atlanta, so I decided to quit my job to focus on a full-time job search.

For the first time in my life, I was unemployed. Initially, I wasn't worried at all. I thought I'd find a job quickly. I had a good network in New York, and there are so many ad agencies in the city, I figured I'd have a job within a few weeks.

I "temporarily" moved in with my parents in New Jersey so I could live rent-free while I found my next gig. It was January 2004, and I was hard at work on my job search. Most days I took the train into Manhattan for interviews and networking.

While I had a great sense of urgency, the people and companies I was meeting with did not. I got close on a few opportunities, only to see them fade away.

It was an incredibly frustrating time for me. Before I knew it, three months had gone by and I still didn't have a job. Remember that Seinfeld episode I mentioned earlier? "Bald men, with no jobs and no money, who live with their parents, don't approach strange women."

George had described me perfectly! Geez, I felt like such a loser.

Actually, I did have a girlfriend at the time (to whom I'm now married). She would constantly encourage me, but I could tell she was growing concerned about my lack of job prospects. I don't think she was that interested in dating an unemployed guy.

When I turned 30 in March 2004, she took me to New York for the weekend and threw me a party. For many people, a milestone birthday like your 30th is a great memory, but for me, it was pretty much a nightmare. I didn't want to see any friends because I felt like such a loser without a job. But I went out and pretended to have fun while I was dying on the inside.

After the party, I made a decision: I was going to get a job. I doubled my efforts. I reached out to anyone who would talk to me. I went back to the companies where I worked before business school and tracked down all my old colleagues, many of whom I hadn't spoken with in several years.

Sometimes it's all a matter of timing. I randomly sent a note to a woman who worked in HR at an agency where I used to work. As luck would have it, she had moved to a new company, and they were actively hiring. She put me in touch with the right people, and I got the job.

I have to say, it wasn't exactly the job I was looking for, but it was the right level and the right compensation based on my experience. I started in May that year. It had taken a little over four months to find a job. It felt more like four years, but I was just happy to be employed again.

The whole experience taught me a few good lessons that have stuck with me over time:

1. Stay positive

When you don't have a job, it's very easy to start feeling sorry for yourself. I remember a few days during my search when it was hard to get out of bed in the morning. But you have to stay positive. Remember, you will eventually get a job. It just might take a bit longer than you were expecting. If you're negative, your prospective employers will pick up on that in the interviews, and it may prevent you from getting the job you want.

2. Always be networking

The best way to get a job is through a personal referral. That's why you have to constantly build and maintain your professional network. Don't wait until you need a job to start networking – do it when you have a job. Do it now. I recommend trying to do some kind of networking activity at least once a week. Attend an event or have lunch/coffee with a colleague. The better your network, the easier it will be to find your next gig.

3. Work every angle

When you're looking for a job, you have to cast a wide net. Don't just sit at home and apply for jobs online. You have to hustle. Talk to your network. Talk to recruiters. Talk to the guy sitting next to you at Starbucks. You never know where a hot lead will come from. If you're looking for a job and your calendar is not packed with meetings, you're probably not doing enough.

4. Don't be desperate

During my job search, I had a company make me a total lowball offer. Even though I was eager to get to work, I passed on it. I'm sure I would have done great in the role and I probably would have enjoyed the job. But there was a disconnect between my value and the value that this company was assigning to me. In the end, I'm glad I didn't take the role. It would have been bad to start a job already frustrated with my compensation and title. That frustration would only grow over time and potentially affect my performance.

5. Help other people find jobs

Over the past ten plus years, I've built a pretty good network in the Atlanta marketing community, so I have a lot of people who come to me when they're looking for their next job. I'm always willing to help out if I can, and I know they'll try to help me when I'm ready to find my next adventure.

Like I said, your career will have highs and lows. It's important when you hit that low point to always remember that it's only temporary. The great thing about hitting rock bottom is that there's really only one way to go from there – UP.

Looking for Opportunities to Go Beyond Marketing

As I look back on my career, I feel very fortunate to have been given opportunities that go beyond just marketing functions. Whenever these opportunities have come my way, I've always enthusiastically said "yes." Even though I've known that I may not have the necessary experience or expertise, I've never turned down the

opportunity to expand my portfolio and make a larger impact on the business.

The fact is, when you do a good job in one role, company leadership will usually look for ways to give you more work. As they say, no good deed shall go unpunished.

These new opportunities that come your way indicate that the leadership team trusts and values you as an employee. While it can be daunting at times, I've found that the non-marketing opportunities have been the ones where I've learned the most and made the biggest impact.

When I joined PGi in 2012, my boss, Ed Trimble, asked me to meet him for breakfast on my first day. We met at the Flying Biscuit in Buckhead, located next to the PGi headquarters in the Terminus building at the corner of Peachtree and Piedmont. As we ate our eggs and grits, Ed let me know that he was giving me a sales team to manage. His theory was that since I was responsible for marketing campaigns to drive leads, I should also be responsible for the sales team that had to convert those leads into revenue.

You have to be kidding me, I thought. I had never worked in sales. I had never managed a sales team before. I really don't know what Ed was thinking. But on your first day of a new job, you're not in a position to push back on your boss. So, I confidently agreed to take on the responsibility, while I was pretty concerned on the inside.

As I dove into my sales leadership duties, I found that while the specific responsibilities were different, a lot of the core skills I used as a marketing leader transferred well to this sales role. First, I had to define the problems that existed and then come up with solutions. Second, I had to build the right team. Third, I had to track our results and look for opportunities to get better.

One of the keys for me was finding a good sales manager I could rely on. As someone with limited sales experience, I needed that righthand man at my side. Fortunately, a guy named Drew Prante raised his hand when he found out about this new sales team I'd be managing. Drew was an awesome partner in crime. He really understood the sales process and took the day-to-day team management off my plate so I could focus more on strategy than execution. He also helped me identify and recruit some of the company's top sellers to join our team. Once we had the right people in place, good things started to happen.

I found that managing sales and marketing together was a good thing. I had to take a much more critical look at the leads marketing was generating for sales to make sure they were converting into real opportunities. You can't just blame the sales team for not closing the marketing leads if you're responsible for that team's performance. I had to facilitate a lot more collaboration between the two functions to ensure we were all on the same page.

It ended up being a great thing. The sales and marketing teams really bonded and worked incredibly well together. Our sales manager and marketing director would talk to each other multiple times a day to ensure lead quality was good and strong prospects were followed up with as quickly as possible.

Over the next three years, that sales team would absolutely crush it. They all ended up making a lot more money than they were making before I joined. Every year, several team members would be among the top sales reps in the entire company, earning their way to the coveted "President's Club" trip to a super fancy One and Only Resort. I personally never got to go on those swanky trips, but I was always glad to see my team members go.

It can be daunting to be given responsibilities outside your core competency. But if you approach it with the right attitude and commit to figuring it out, you can make an even bigger impact on the company than you ever thought possible. It also gives you the confidence to take on more work and constantly expand your portfolio.

When I joined QASymphony, I was given a team of sales development reps (SDRs) to manage. Then at ParkMobile, I was asked to take on the Head of Product role in addition to my marketing responsibilities. These expanded duties have made me a better marketer because they've exposed me to different parts of the business and, in some ways, helped evolve my thinking about what marketing has to do.

So don't confine yourself to the "marketing box." Look for opportunities to take on new projects that go beyond the marketing function. Have a talk with your boss about expanding your portfolio. Do a rotation in a different department to learn a new part of the business. All of this will make you better at your job as a marketer and enable you to make a bigger impact on the company.

Play Nice with Others

Building a Strong Peer Network

I firmly believe that one of the most valuable things I've built in my career is a strong peer network. Having this network of accomplished professionals I've known for many years has helped me find jobs, find employees, and get better at everything I do.

I didn't just join one of those "CMO groups." I proactively sought out the marketers and business leaders I wanted to get to know. I made it a point to keep in touch with people I met at conferences and events. I invested the time to get to know them over coffees, lunches, and drinks after work. Many of these people have become my good friends.

In 2020, I had the opportunity to teach an MBA class at Emory University's Goizueta school. As I put together the course curriculum, I reached out to my network to line up guest speakers. The response from my peers was pretty amazing. All of them wanted to participate in some way. The class ended up being a fantastic lineup of marketing leaders and successful entrepreneurs, so each session was almost like a mini-TED Talk.

In one of the classes, I brought in four CMOs to discuss how they navigated their careers to make it to the C-suite. It was a great discussion. In the middle of it, I realized many of us had helped each other land our current roles. In fact, one of the panelists, Leigh Segall, CMO of Smart Communications, had actually introduced me to the leadership team at ParkMobile when they were doing their CMO search. That's how I got my foot in the door.

In my previous job at QASymphony, I was introduced to the CEO by Sangram Vajre, the Co-Founder of Terminus. Sangram had talked to QASymphony about the open CMO position and ended up passing on it, but suggested that I pursue it. It ended up being a great fit for me, and I had a great run there as we grew the company from a $1 million business to a $20 million business and raised $50 million in venture funding along the way.

It's pretty amazing to think that I got my last two jobs directly through my network connections. I'm sure the companies that hired me appreciated that they didn't have to pay the high fees of an executive recruiter.

In turn, I'm always trying to help many of my peers find their next adventure. If I hear of open roles, I'll make the connection if there's a good fit. It's a virtuous cycle. We all help each other advance our careers.

Beyond your career, having a strong peer network can help when it comes to building your team. When I started my job at ParkMobile, I needed to bring in some key people to build out the marketing department. I immediately reached out to my network with the positions I needed to fill. I ended up bringing on two people I'd worked with at previous companies. A third person was referred through my peer network. These three people formed the foundation of our new marketing team, which we continued to build on. Since I was able to find them all without an external recruiter, I saved the company tens of thousands of dollars, plus I was able to get them up and running fast. So rather than spending six months finding the needle in a haystack, I had my team assembled fast and ready to rock.

I'm very proud that most of my team today at ParkMobile was sourced either through my network or the networks of people on the team.

Another benefit of the peer network is information sharing. With all the marketing technology, agency vendors, and advertising options to choose from, it's crucial to get unbiased opinions on what works and what doesn't. For example, if you're buying a new marketing automation software, the vendor will always provide client references. These references can be helpful, but they're probably not going to give you the full story.

Before making any big investment decisions, I always ping my network to see what experience people have had with a specific vendor. It helps validate that you're making the right decision, and more importantly, can help you avoid a potential disaster. In one case, I was close to signing a six-figure contract with a marketing technology vendor when I discovered that someone in my peer group had had a terrible experience with them. It turns out this vendor made a lot of big promises but couldn't deliver. I ended up backing out of the deal as a result, and I'm glad I did.

How to build a strong peer network

When I talk about my peer network, people often say, "That sounds great, Jeff, but how do you really do it? It doesn't sound like something I can do." Or they say, "I just don't have time."

Well, I'd argue that building a peer network is not hard to do and doesn't have to take up too much time. You just have to commit to it.

I allocate time each week to nurturing my network. I'm continually looking at my list of peers and checking in with those I haven't heard from in a while. I try to block off a few dates every month for lunches and coffees with the people in my network. I've even heard of some people using a CRM tool to manage their professional network. I personally haven't taken that step yet, but I think it's a pretty good idea.

I'm always looking to expand my network, so I spend time going to events where marketers gather. This is a great way to meet new people to add to your peer group. It also can be a lot of fun.

Five things you can do right now to build your peer network:

1. Join a local marketing organization. Every city has them. You may have to pay a small fee, but it will be worth it. Once you join, get involved. Serve on a committee or take a leadership role. This will help you meet more people in the organization.
2. Find your peers. Spend time on LinkedIn looking for people just like you. Same level, same title, same industry. Reach out to them. Offer to meet up and buy them a coffee.
3. Share your thoughts on marketing. When you put yourself out there, people will be drawn to you. Post some of your marketing thoughts, ideas, challenges, and questions on social media. Then engage with the people who engage with your content.
4. Identify the influencers. Every marketing community has influencers. These are the people everyone seems to know. Make sure you know who those influencers are and become part of their circle.
5. Ask for help. If you have a challenge you're dealing with, ask the community for support. Maybe you have a position you're struggling to fill or a campaign that's not working. Post the question to the community and see what comes back. You might be surprised how many people are willing to help out.

I view having a strong network as part of my job. And like every other aspect of a job, you just have to spend time doing it. I promise you, over time it will pay off.

Good Lessons from a Bad Boss

In my career, I've been pretty lucky to have had some great bosses – bosses who have really mentored me and helped me grow. But, like most people, I've also had a few bad ones. It's really tough to have a bad boss. It makes it hard to walk into work every day.

When I look back at my bad boss experiences, I have to admit that I learned a lot. To be honest, I probably learned more lessons from my bad bosses than the good ones.

You see, the value of having a bad boss is that they teach you what not to do when it comes to your job and how to manage your employees. Sometimes, knowing what not to do is almost as valuable as knowing what to do.

Here's my list of "don'ts" I learned from a bad boss.

1. Don't be insecure

It's great to have talented people on your team. As a boss of emerging rock stars, you may have a tendency to be a bit insecure at times; it might feel like your reports are outshining you. But as a leader, it's critical that you don't feel threatened. Instead, embrace it. Having a great team is actually a sign that you're doing something right as the boss. Give your talented employees the opportunity to shine and let that reflect on you.

2. Don't forget to give credit where credit is due

People generally like to be recognized if they do good work. Whenever you have a chance, give the people on your team a shoutout. Talk about their accomplishments. Brag about them in front of their peers and executives. It will make your team feel great, and it will also make you look good as the boss. It shows that you don't take credit for other people's work – that you'd rather give up the spotlight. You'll look like a strong, confident leader to your superiors, and it will help you build stronger relationships with the people on your team.

3. Don't let issues fester

I had one boss who had some issues with me, but he would never address them with me directly. Instead, he would let those issues fester over long periods of time, then usually out of nowhere, he would just unload on me. He would bring things up that had happened many months ago. There were times when I didn't even remember what he was talking about. He would say things like, "Remember when we were in that meeting and you cut me off mid-sentence?"

Obviously, I did something that really bothered him at the time, and when he would finally confront me, it was just awful. This taught me that you have to address issues with your employees when they happen. The longer you wait, the more frustrated you'll get. As frustration grows, the likely outcome of the eventual conversation with the employee will worsen. And it's really not fair to your employee. You're much better off having more frequent conversations than letting things build up into one epic thrashing.

4. Don't get upset if your employees want to explore other opportunities in the company

There will come a time when someone who works for you will be ready for a change. People want to grow their careers and get new experiences. They can't always do that in their current role. The bad boss will be upset by this and may even see it as a betrayal. The bad boss won't lift a finger to help you find a new role. On the other hand, the good boss will be supportive, and may even help you find that new position within the company. The good boss knows that your value to the company goes beyond your current role.

5. Don't treat employees badly if they leave for another job

I'd worked for a company for several years. I was generally happy in my job, but I'd had a great opportunity presented to me, so I decided to make a move. When I resigned, my boss was furious. He basically didn't even acknowledge me for my last two weeks on the job. He really left me with a horrible feeling about him and the company I was leaving. That was a shame because I'd had a rewarding experience working there. Now when employees leave my team (which fortunately doesn't happen very often), I really try to treat them well out the door. I want them to feel like they were appreciated. Maybe they'll come back someday. Or at least, they'll speak highly of their experience at the company, which could help attract a good candidate to replace them.

6. Don't be a jerk

I'm sure there are people who have worked for me in the past who may not have great things to say. But in general, I hope just about everyone who has worked for me will say that I'm a pretty nice guy and I wasn't a jerk to them. People probably spend too much time at work. It's a huge part of a person's life. That's why you have to treat your co-workers with respect. You don't want to be the person they have to work for; you want to be the one they want to work for.

So if you're working for a "bad boss," hang in there. It won't last forever. And you'll learn some valuable lessons that may actually make you a better manager in the future.

Navigate Job Changes

Anytime you make a job change, there are a lot of things to consider. Blindly jumping from job to job is not a smart way to manage your career. Here's a useful exercise for anyone considering a job change.

Key Questions to Ask Yourself:

» What did I like about past jobs?

» What are the things I didn't like?

» What kind of people do I want to be around? More serious or more fun? More introverted or more extroverted?

» What kind of companies or teams do I like working in? Large or small?

» What stage is the company in? Startup, growth, or mature?

» Do I want to build things from the ground up or take things already built and make them better?

» What kind of product or service do I want to work on? Consumer or business? Simple or technical?

» How good (or bad) is the product you'll be working on?

» What kind of marketing budget does the company have?

» What are the expectations of marketing?

» What industry does the company operate in? Is it an industry I'm interested in?

» What are the dynamics of the company ownership? Public or private? Founder owned or venture funded? Who is on the board?

There are many more questions you can ask yourself. For me, the questions above helped me develop a framework for the kind of opportunity I wanted as I transitioned from one marketing job to another. As I started to go through each one, I wrote down my answers, which helped me clarify what I was looking for.

My Sample Answers

What I'm looking for:

- » Opportunity in a small- to mid-sized high-growth technology company
- » Ideally, this company would create a B2B or B2C product that I would understand on a deep level, since I would be a user of it
- » The product would be going after a large market and clearly address an unmet need for the target audience
- » Product has some differentiated competitive advantage in the market
- » I want to be in a highly engaged and collaborative culture where employees like to work together
- » I want to build something great, and I'm not afraid to roll up my sleeves and get in the weeds
- » I want to work in an industry where I have a strong interest
- » I would have the resources required to build a marketing team and program
- » There would be higher risk/reward, meaning I would have the opportunity to get performance-based incentives (bonuses, equity)

Just as important, what I am not looking for:

- » A large company that is very bureaucratic with too many layers
- » A company that is at a mature stage (not growing)
- » A culture that is more serious and introverted
- » Product issues and/or lack of product innovation
- » Lower risk/reward – compensation with limited financial upside

Watch out for:

» The relationship between the board and the CEO
» Toxic culture issues
» Dysfunction at the executive level
» Unrealistic expectations for marketing
» Constant churn in the position you're taking on

This framework has been a valuable tool for helping me evaluate opportunities in my career. It also helps me craft questions that I ask during the interview process. I have passed on a few jobs that met a lot of my criteria because they checked too many boxes on the "watch out" list.

Your framework will likely be very different from mine. That doesn't matter. The important thing is that you get it down on paper so you have a good way to evaluate the opportunities in front of you. Hopefully, you won't change jobs that often in your career, but you have to get it right when you do, and having a framework to guide your decisions will help.

KEY TAKEAWAYS

» Frequent job change is the new normal for marketers. That's why it's important for marketing professionals to develop a strong personal brand.
» You need to focus on your personal brand, because if you don't define yourself, someone else will.
» Find forums where you can showcase your skills and experience. Speak at a conference, write a blog, or go on a podcast. You have to be more than just bullet points on a resume.
» If LinkedIn looks just like your resume, you're doing it wrong! Use LinkedIn to tell the story of your career journey and position yourself for the job you want. Use multi-media assets to showcase your work

and make sure your headline truly reflects your personal brand.

» There are proven links between physical fitness and job performance. Make time in your busy week to work out.

» You have to make sure the company you're working for is the right fit for you. You don't want to have to change who you are when you go to work every day.

» After a job interview, write a thank-you email!

» Before leaving your current job, make sure you get answers to all your questions about your prospective employer and talk to your peers and mentors to ensure you're making the right choice.

» You will inevitably hit some low points in your career. When that happens, just remember, it's only temporary; things will eventually turn around.

» As you build your career, look for opportunities to expand your portfolio beyond marketing. Having different experiences will make you a better marketer and enable you to have a bigger impact on the company.

» Devote time and energy to building a strong peer network. Whether you're hiring new employees or trying to find a new job, having a strong network will pay big dividends for you in your career.

» Before making a job change, figure out what you're looking for in a new job, what you're not looking for, and identify any potential red flags with your new employer (do the exercise in **"Navigate Job Changes" on page 87**).

PART 4: ASSEMBLE A BIGGER & BETTER BAND

Better Together

Like many rock stars, Bruce Springsteen was inducted into the Rock and Roll Hall of Fame in 1999. However, he was inducted as a solo artist. This was very controversial because he rose to fame playing with the E Street Band. Many felt they should have all been inducted together, and that Bruce should not have accepted the award as a solo artist.

Fast forward to 2014: the E Street Band finally got inducted into the Rock and Roll Hall of Fame. In his speech inducting the band, Bruce said this:

> "I told a story with the E Street Band that was, and is, bigger than I ever could have told on my own. And I believe that settles that question.
>
> But that is the hallmark of a rock and roll band – the narrative you tell together is bigger than anyone could have told on your own. That's the Rolling Stones; the Sex Pistols; that's Bob Marley and the Wailers. That's James Brown and His Famous Flames. That's Neil Young and Crazy Horse.
>
> So, I thank you my beautiful men and women of E Street. You made me dream and love bigger than I could have ever without you."[12]

Bruce's message is clear: his success was propelled by the band he had around him.

I think about building marketing teams similarly. When I started moving up into a management role, I quickly learned

---

12. Rolling Stone. "Read Bruce Springsteen's E Street Band Induction Speech." *Rolling Stone*, 11 Apr. 2014, www.rollingstone.com/music/music-news/read-bruce-springsteens-e-street-band-induction-speech-242289.

that my success had less to do with me and more to do with how good a team I could build around me.

In Jay Elliott's book *Leading Apple with Steve Jobs*, Jobs makes the statement: "I noticed that the dynamic range between what an average person could accomplish and what the best person could accomplish was 50 or 100 to 1... A small team of A+ players can run circles around a giant team of B and C players."

Steve Jobs was right about a lot of things, but I think he's really right about hiring A+ players.

At a previous job, I was brought in to lead a marketing team, and most of the key players were already in place. As I transitioned into the business, I quickly realized we didn't have the right people. In some cases, they didn't have the skills; in other cases, they didn't have enough experience. Some just didn't have the right attitude.

Unfortunately, I was a bit slow to make a change, so I would just end up doing people's work for them. This went on for several months until I reached a breaking point. I was overwhelmed and not getting anything done.

I talked to my boss about it and explained the situation. He immediately said I should fire the people who weren't working out and bring in better people. I agreed but suggested that maybe we should give them one more chance.

"Jeff," he said, "I've never fired someone and then said that I wished I'd waited longer."

That's good advice. So I made the decision to let a few people on the team go. I knew it would make my job more challenging in the near term, but it was the right thing to do for the company.

Over the next few months, I was able to recruit a few new people to the team who were total rock stars. Once they got up and running, they took a ton of work off my plate. Suddenly we were executing at a much higher level than ever before. They helped me get out of the weeds so I could focus on more of the strategic planning.

These people were the critical pieces of the band that I was missing. Once they were in place, we were rocking! Just like Springsteen, having the right band made me better than I could ever be on my own.

How to Build the Band

Here are some things being said at this very moment in marketing departments all around the globe:

» We need some new ideas
» We have to think outside the box
» We have to break the paradigm
» What got us here won't get us where we want to be

Sound familiar? You've probably heard someone say things like this, or maybe you've even said it yourself. It seems there's universal acknowledgement that the current state is never good enough. You have to continue to change, grow, adapt, and innovate.

Recognizing the need for new ideas is the easy part. The hard part is figuring out what to do about it.

I've spoken about this with many colleagues, and we generally agree that when you need new ideas, oftentimes you have to look outside your organization. You have to bring in talent that will infuse new ideas into your company.

But that's not always an easy task.

When it comes to recruiting, companies tend to think too narrowly about the kinds of candidates they want. Just look at any job board out there, and you'll see a list of "musts":

» Must have eight years of experience
» Must have an MBA
» Must have category experience
» Must have B2B marketing experience

These requirements actually screen out the kind of big thinkers that companies want to recruit, so you just end up seeing the same kinds of candidates. And then guess what happens? You end up hiring the same kinds of people with the same old ideas.

Then you sit around and wonder, "Why aren't we moving the business forward? Why aren't we growing revenue?"

Then maybe you fire the ad agency. Maybe the CMO loses his or her job. But you never get the new Big Ideas that you're looking for.

What do you do about this?

Well, I don't claim to know everything about anything. I'm a generalist who's had a career that has given me broad experience across brands and categories, B2B and B2C, traditional and digital, client- and agency-side.

Despite being a generalist, I have had great success over my career assembling high-performing teams that helped build brands, enable a sales force, and grow revenue.

I think the key to our success has had everything to do with the kinds of people we bring onto the team. We've hired people who don't fit a set mold, people who didn't have traditional experience working in a specific industry.

I don't mean to disparage people who are specialists or subject matter experts. There are many industries that probably require a specialized skill set. But there are also many that don't, where learning curves are less steep and general marketing skills are easily transferable.

When we hire, we look for what I call "marketing rock stars." These are people who are more generalists than specialists. Their experiences are very broad, so they bring lots of different ideas to the table. They're creative. They're collaborative. They have the ability to stretch.

Most of all, they have no preconceived notions of the "formula" to solve a specific business problem. They're able to look at the challenge, develop a strategy, and then bring a complete arsenal of marketing tactics to help solve that problem. Many times, they bring ideas from different fields that we can transfer to our company.

If you really want new ideas, you have to hire people who actually have new ideas. And you won't find a top-notch marketing rock star with a standard job description.

Hire Fast

I've done a lot of recruiting over the years. One key lesson I've learned is that in this competitive market, you have to move fast. The conventional wisdom used to be "hire slow, fire fast" and I definitely believed it. In the past, I would be cautious when making a hire. I wanted to get it right so I would usually do extensive interviewing, have the candidate come in and meet the entire team, check references, and more.

But recently I'd noticed my process was causing me to miss out on some good candidates. I'd be ready to move forward with an offer, only to find the candidate had just accepted a job at another company. This happened to me several times recently.

Atlanta is a very hot market right now, and it seems like every company out there is hiring, so it's becoming harder to find top talent. I got tired of being "left at the altar," so I adjusted my strategy and increased the pace of the recruiting process. If I like a candidate who is actively talking to other companies, I'll quickly move forward with an offer – even a verbal offer on the spot after the interview.

I found out one recent candidate was about to interview with the CMO of another company, so I moved fast to get an offer in front of her before that interview. She ended up cancelling the interview with the other CMO and accepted the job.

Another strategy is to find the talent before they're actually "on the market." Recently, I was in the audience at an event for a technology accelerator called Techstars, and they played a video about the organization's team. They featured a woman with the title "Content and Brand Strategy." At the time, I was actively searching for someone with that kind of skillset. I looked her up on LinkedIn and sent her a message asking if she would be interested in learning about ParkMobile. A few days later, we met for lunch, and we quickly made her an offer. From the day I met her to the job offer, the entire process took only about two weeks.

In this competitive job market, you have to move fast. Great candidates won't be on the market long, but you can find those candidates before they even start looking for a job.

Bringing the Band Together

You've assembled the band. You have all the right pieces in place. But how do you turn a group of individual contributors into a band that goes on stage and rocks out in front of an audience of 30,000 screaming fans?

Just hiring the right people does not guarantee you will have a strong team. As the leader, you have to invest time and energy into bringing that team together and making sure the sum is greater than the parts. How do you do that? Let's explore some strategies to build high-performing teams.

Understanding Different Communication Styles

As a leader you need to learn to understand the people on your team, but you also need to make sure the people on your team really understand each other. A great way to do this is through a personality test. I personally have had great success with the DISC assessment. I've also done the Birkman and Myers-Briggs. These tests provide unique insights about the people on your team and help you understand communication styles, motivations, and more. These assessments have helped me understand how to manage and communicate with my direct reports, and they also show team members how to interact with each other.

There are many professional facilitators who can administer these tests and run a session with the team to explain the findings. It's always very eye-opening to see your team members receive their reports and learn things about themselves they might not have known.

In a previous job, I did the DISC assessment with the sales team I was managing. The DISC basically puts people into four key quadrants based on communication style:

» Dominance: Direct, results-oriented, firm, strong-willed, forceful
» Influence: Outgoing, enthusiastic, optimistic, high-spirited, lively
» Conscientiousness: Analytical, reserved, precise, private, systematic
» Steadiness: Even-tempered, accommodating, patient, humble, tactful

As expected, most of the salespeople were in either the "Dominance" or "Influence" quadrants in the test. This is pretty typical with salespeople. They tend to be more aggressive, outgoing, and extroverted. They all like to talk over each other. When you're around a group of salespeople, you often feel like you're fighting for airtime.

Interestingly, one sales rep was in the "C" quadrant (Conscientiousness). He was much quieter than the rest of the team, but he was very effective. In fact, he was at the top of the leaderboard, generating the most revenue that year. The reason was that as a "C" he was a much better listener than the other reps; many of the "D" and "I" reps would spend an entire sales call talking at their prospects. The "C" rep would ask probing questions and let his prospects do the talking.

As a team, we talked about what this meant for our dynamic. The "D" and "I" reps realized that they would have to do more to include the "C" rep in team conversations. As one person said, "He's not just going to jump in and tell us what he thinks. But if we ask him questions and bring him into the conversation, he'll have really good things to say."

This was eye-opening for everyone and really helped us as a team. We better understood that not all people communicate in the same way, and we learned how to do a better job communicating with each other. Many of the "D" and "I" reps were also more aware of their tendency to steamroll conversations. The "C" rep learned that he had to do more to speak up and make sure his voice was heard in team meetings.

Overall, doing the DISC assessment really helped bring us together as a team and improved the way we communicated with each other.

Getting Below the Surface

In the past, I've worked on teams where it was all business all the time. You didn't really get to know your co-workers. People were really guarded. There was a wall between the personal and the professional.

I totally understand employees not wanting to bring their personal baggage to work. But it's important to remember that most of us spend the vast majority of our week with our co-workers. That's a lot of time to be with people who aren't your good friends or family. And if you don't take the time to get to know each other, your work environment (where you spend eight or more hours a day) probably won't be very fun. We all have to go to work every day. You might as well go someplace where you enjoy being around the people.

From what I've found, teams that are more open with each other are higher performing. You feel connected at a much deeper level. You want to support each other because you see your team members as real people, not just boxes on an org chart.

One exercise I've done at team offsites is having everyone bring in a 1-page photo collage that illustrates themselves. Whenever I do this, I'm always amazed by what I learn about the people I'm working with. People share their hobbies and interests and tell stories about their friends and family. Sometimes it can get a bit emotional, but it is a great way to build team unity.

Celebrating Wins

As a leader, it's important not to get so focused on what's next that you lose track of the here and now. Personally, I'm not one to spend a lot of time patting myself on the back when I do something good, because I'm always thinking about all the other stuff we need to do. But you need to take time to celebrate wins with the team. Whether you launch a new campaign or finish a big project, take a moment to recognize the people who made it happen and the hard work that went into it. Take the team out for a special lunch or happy hour to celebrate. Ask the CEO to send a note to the team. Get a commemorative gift to recognize the accomplishment. It will make the team feel great and motivated to move on to the next big thing.

Creating a Safe Space

I've worked with companies in the past where you were not supposed to speak up. If you had an idea, you kept it to yourself and maybe shared it with your direct manager at the right time. If you disagreed with someone, even if you had solid rationale, you wouldn't dare say anything or run the risk of being labeled a "problem employee." These were some of the most toxic and low-performing teams I've been a part of in my career.

I've learned that to be a high-performing team, you need to create an environment where people feel like they can share their ideas and feedback. They know it's not just okay to speak up, it's expected. If you don't say something, that's the problem.

To create this kind of environment, leaders have to push the team to come to the table as active participants, not passive observers. Show your team that you not only want to hear their input and feedback, but you truly value it. When people speak up, encourage them by saying something like "that's a great idea" or "that's really valuable input." Even when they disagree with the team, make sure they know how helpful their feedback is. The more comfortable team members get with participation and engagement, the higher performing the team gets.

We've talked about a few ways you can really turn an average bar band into a rock band that's packing arenas around the country. Now let's talk about how that rock band needs to work and collaborate effectively to get stuff done with other departments in the organization.

Playing Nice

Every organization has bottlenecks; sometimes they come in the form of your senior leadership. Sometimes bottlenecks can actually be a good thing because they keep you from making impulsive decisions that could potentially hurt the business or waste money. But when your marketing program sucks, bottlenecks could be disastrous to your progress.

At PGi we had just relaunched our website. One of my goals was to improve our conversion rates. We had a lot of visitors to our site, but they just weren't turning into leads for the sales team. I'd been reading about companies having success with live chat on their website and thought that could be a great way to better engage with our site visitors.

I started evaluating the options available, but soon the IT department found out and approached me about it. They were also looking at live chat technology, but they needed something that could be used across the enterprise. They asked me to wait for them to complete their work and then use the technology that they selected.

I had some concerns about how long this would take, but they assured me that

it was going to be a fast process because this was a huge priority for the organization.

Now, I didn't probe on what "fast" meant to our IT team; I just assumed it meant fast. That assumption was a big mistake. I learned that the definition of "fast" differs greatly between marketing and IT.

Weeks went by without any progress. Every time I would check in, the IT lead would tell me that they were still building out their business requirements. When they finally started the vendor evaluation, three months had already gone by. I was growing increasingly irritated with my IT team.

Finally, IT started the formal evaluation. They had several chat vendors visit our office and make extensive presentations. After another three months, they made the technical selection of a chat vendor. I was very excited we could finally get going and put chat on the website.

I called the IT lead and asked him when we could get up and running with chat. "Hold on Jeff," he said. "We just finished the technical selection. Now we have to go through the procurement process, and then we'll start the implementation process. It will be at least another three months before we can get started."

I was silent for a second. Then – and I'm not proud of it – I just unloaded on this poor IT guy. I don't remember exactly what I said, but I believe there were several F-bombs involved. I was so mad. These guys had promised me "fast," but now it was going to be a full nine months from the time we first discussed live chat before we could even get started. And I didn't believe it was going to be another three months – this was going to take much longer. Getting through our procurement department was no easy feat.

This entire situation was just unacceptable to me. I needed to drive results. I needed more leads. And these IT guys were the bottleneck.

So I took out my corporate card, went online, and bought a chat tool called Olark. I spent the afternoon training myself on it and connecting it with Salesforce. The next day,

I trained my inbound sales team to use it and pushed it live on the website.

The entire process took about eight hours, and I had live chat up and running on the website. Eight hours! I had been waiting six months for IT to help me with this, but they just couldn't deliver.

Looking back, I understand now that marketing and IT people think much differently about things. IT people are generally rule followers; they are risk averse and like process. They are thinking more about security and scalability than business results. Marketers are rule breakers. We like speed, and we want to do things that will drive the business forward. You can clearly see that disconnect at play in this story.

Once we got chat up on the website, the impact was immediate. Our sales guys were fielding a good volume of chat conversations every day. Because we hooked chat up with Salesforce, we could track all the leads and revenue associated with chat. Within the first six months, we generated about $200,000 of revenue directly sourced from chat. The chat tool cost me about $1200 for the year. How's that for an ROI?

And whatever happened to that IT chat initiative? Well, it wasn't a happy ending. After the technical selection, the deal got stuck in procurement for several more months. A few of the IT people who were leading the initiative ended up leaving the company, so the evaluation got passed along to another team that didn't have time for it. Eventually, the initiative died. All those hours wasted.

This whole ordeal was an important learning experience. It taught me that you can't just wait around for people with completely different priorities to help you get what you need. You have to take matters into your own hands.

If I'd waited another six months for IT to provide a chat tool, the company would have potentially lost out on $200,000 of revenue and I might have been out of a job. I still kick myself that I didn't just implement chat sooner – that

$200,000 could have been $400,000 if I had implemented chat back when I initially wanted to.

By breaking through a bottleneck, I was able to make a tangible impact on our business. Yes, some of the IT team were upset by what I did, but once they saw the results, they couldn't argue. I did have to spend some time working to repair that relationship, and I still feel bad about taking my frustrations out on them. To their credit, this incident led to some soul searching for our IT team. They became less rigid in their processes and let marketing try out more technologies. They looked at this as a good way to do a proof of concept before rolling out tools across the enterprise. I'm proud to say that after this incident, we formed a much stronger partnership.

It's important to recognize that bottlenecks exist in every organization, big or small. For marketers to be successful, you have to identify bottlenecks that are impeding your progress and do everything you can to avoid them.

Think the Sales Team Doesn't Get It? Maybe You Don't Get It.

Back in 2007, I started working on the marketing team at AutoTrader.com. At the time, there was a big wall between the sales and marketing organizations. We would sit in our corporate office, look out at our sales team and say, "They just don't get it."

Then I had an opportunity to spend some time in the field. Talking to one of our more outspoken sales reps, I asked him what he thought about the marketing department. Without even thinking, he said, "You guys just don't get it."

I'm sure this sounds familiar. The field thinks corporate doesn't get it. Corporate thinks the field doesn't get it.

Well, at least we agree on something.

The thing is, both sides are probably right to some extent. People sitting in a corporate office really can't understand the day-to-day pain a sales rep has to endure. Similarly, a sales rep working independently out in the field probably has little understanding of the bureaucratic complexities in a corporate office.

As a marketer, I view the sales force as my client. One of my key responsibilities is to provide them with the tools they need to be successful. So if my client thinks I "don't get it," then I have a big problem.

Our marketing team set out on a journey to "get it." We got out of the office and started spending a lot of time in the field. We went on sales ride-alongs, attended local sales meetings, and listened to our sales reps and their customers. We immersed ourselves in the sales organization.

And you know what? We actually started to get it. Our marketing materials got better and started to reflect the issues we saw in the field. As we tracked the adoption of those new marketing materials by our sales reps, we saw that usage dramatically increased.

Then we took it a step further. We formed a sales advisory board and brought ten of our best reps to our corporate office for a three-day work session. The result? A complete overhaul of all our marketing materials to make them more relevant and more useful for the field. These new marketing materials were built for the sales force, by the sales force.

That sales advisory board started meeting every quarter, and even though I'm no longer at the company, it continues to this day. Sales and marketing work together to develop new and innovative ways to support the field. We also had a little fun along the way. One advisory board event featured skeeball, karaoke, and helicopter tours of Atlanta. Our advisory board actually became quite the status symbol for the sales force. One of the most common questions I used to get from the field was, "How can I get on that advisory board?"

The best part of "getting it" was that we saw a clear link between the enhancement in our marketing support and the overall performance of the sales organization. After we started making some changes based on feedback from the field, we saw AutoTrader.com revenue go way up, customer satisfaction reached an all-time high, and customer churn hit an all-time low.

I'm not going to suggest that marketing gets all the credit for that. But let's just say it's a nice coincidence.

> Stop complaining and start collaborating. To be successful, sales and marketing have to work together.

Marketing needs to listen, to understand what the sales force needs. The sales force needs to get more involved with what goes on at headquarters and help the marketing folks understand what they need to be successful. We all have skin in this game.

I remember attending a sales meeting a few years after we really started to collaborate together. I gave a presentation on our marketing support for the year. Guess what happened? A standing ovation. After the meeting, the same rep who'd told me four years ago, "You don't get it," approached me. He patted me on the back and said, "Hey, you're finally starting to get it! It's about time." Well, no one said perceptions were easy to change. But we were making progress.

Your Unlikely Ally: the CFO

There's definitely a healthy tension between the finance and marketing departments. A CMO I know refers to his CFO as the "CF-No."

You can understand why. Marketing's job is to make strategic investments to build the brand and grow the business. Often these investments are really expensive and can be hard to measure.

The CFO's job is to responsibly manage the company's money. The CFO wants to make sure every penny spent is worth it. When it comes to marketing, a CFO will want to understand what the company is getting back from this investment.

A few years back, I was working at a technology company where finance and marketing hardly ever spoke. Finance had no idea what marketing was doing with the company's money. So if the company needed money because we weren't hitting our numbers, they would just take it out of the marketing budget, no questions asked.

As a marketing leader, this is problematic. If your budget keeps getting cut, you can't execute your program. If you can't execute your program, you won't deliver for the business. If you don't deliver, you'll probably lose your job.

One day we had a meeting with the finance team to review expenses and forecasted spend. One of the finance people was asking questions about our spend with Google. It was a big number, so he wanted to understand what we were doing with that money.

We pulled up some reports to show our spend on Google and the impact on our business. Over the past six months, we had dramatically improved our results in search engines, reducing cost per click and increasing conversions. We were also starting to see real revenue produced through our Google spend.

The finance guy looked at our data and was shocked. He said, "So you can actually track this stuff?" Our marketing team looked at each other, surprised by what we were hearing. Of course we could track it. We tracked it fanatically. We were obsessed with improving our results.

But we never shared this with our finance team. As far as they knew, we were just throwing money in the fireplace. After the meeting, it dawned on us: we have to do a better job educating the finance people about what we're doing in marketing. Finance people like data. Our marketing team had a lot of data on the performance of our program, but we weren't sharing it.

I think a lot of marketers fall into this trap. They are hesitant to share results with the finance department. But if you don't help finance understand what you are doing, if you make marketing a "black box," your budget will inevitably get cut. On the other hand, if you work to build trust with the CFO and finance team, you might actually get to keep your budget, and in some cases, get more budget.

Take it from me, here are some things to NEVER tell your CFO:

- » "You just have to trust me."
- » "There's no possible way to track ROI on that investment."
- » "I don't know if it works or not."
- » "You have to spend money to make money."
- » "We're spending on brand awareness. You can't measure that."

To have a successful relationship with the CFO, marketing needs to be transparent. Show your work. Your CFO does not expect you to be perfect. They won't cut your budget just because one campaign didn't work, but you have to explain why it didn't work and what you are doing to fix it.

My marketing team started doing monthly check-ins with our finance team. We always came prepared with data to show the value of what we were doing with the company money. After several months, the finance team really started to get it. They asked good questions. They learned the meaning of a lot of our marketing vocabulary. And most importantly, they understood what we were spending marketing dollars on and why it was important for the business.

I remember at one point about four weeks before the end of the quarter, the company was tracking well behind our forecasted expenses. Our finance team could have just taken

5 THINGS to NEVER! tell your C.F.O.

"YOU JUST HAVE TO TRUST ME!"

"il don't know if it works or not."

"THERE'S NO POSSIBLE WAY TO TRACK R.O.I. ON THAT INVESTMENT."

"You have to spend money to make money!"

"WE'RE SPENDING ON BRAND AWARENESS. YOU CAN'T MEASURE THAT!"

that money and added it back to the bottom line. But in this case, our finance team came to me and said, "Jeff, we may have some extra money this quarter. Do you think you could use it for marketing?"

I was in shock. That was a first for me – the finance team actually telling marketing to spend more money! The point is that we built trust with finance that we were spending company money wisely. We showed them that the money invested in marketing would actually generate revenue for the business.

If you're not working closely with the CFO and your finance team, you need to work on that relationship. The best marketing teams can turn the "CF-No" into an ally.

The CMO and CEO Relationship

One of the most challenging relationships for any marketing leader to manage is the one with the CEO. In general, CEOs are very tough. They all have type-A personalities and are driven by results. And most don't come up through the marketing ranks, so they have limited expertise in that area.

CEOs generally come up through the finance, strategy, or operations function. Most CEOs know they need marketing but have a hard time wrapping their heads around it. It's hard to measure in some cases. It takes time and patience to do it right. And it's pretty expensive. You put all that together, and you can understand why marketing leaders often have a bullseye on their back.

As marketers, we often don't do ourselves any favors when it comes to the CEO. I remember being in a meeting with one CEO and sharing some of the results from our digital campaigns. I was bragging about our strong click-through rates, which were well above industry averages. Note that industry averages for digital ads are less than 1% – so if you're doing better than that, you're probably feeling pretty good about yourself. But the CEO looked at that and said, "You're bragging when 99.4% of people are not clicking on your ads?" Point taken.

CEOs will look at every area of the business with a view of winning and losing, growing and declining. When a CEO meets with the head of sales, it's all about who's closing deals and who's not closing deals. If a sales rep doesn't hit their number, that rep will be fired and replaced with a rep who can. If multiple reps aren't hitting their number, then the sales leader will be fired.

For the CEO, marketing is much more difficult to wrap your head around. It's not as black and white as other functions. To some extent, making marketing investments is a leap of faith. You try to make smart investment decisions that will deliver the maximum return, but in the end, it might not work. I think that's why the CMO has the shortest tenure in the C-suite. If the CEO can't measure the impact marketing is having on the organization, eventually they have to make a change.

So what can the CMO do about this?

Set clear expectations

This is key. Too often, marketers will over promise and under deliver. Make sure your CEO really understands what you're doing and how long it will take to deliver results. For example, if you're working on a big initiative around improving your organic search results, make sure the CEO understands that this is not something that will produce results overnight, but in six months you should start to see the impact of the work.

Educate the CEO about marketing

I've found that most CEOs have a very high level of intellectual curiosity. As a marketing leader, you should really take the time to educate the CEO about your marketing program. Explain why you are doing what you are doing. Teach how it works and why it will deliver results for the business. I've found that CEOs really appreciate when you give them a deeper understanding of your expertise. Plus, it helps validate that you do actually know what you're doing.

Turn the CEO's marching orders into objectives

CEOs love to tell you what to do. But if you are just a "yes man" and always do exactly what they tell you to, you may not be doing the right thing for the business. What I've realized is that when CEOs tell you what to do, they're really trying to get you focused on solving a key problem. There could be multiple ways to address it. Since you're the marketing expert, it's incumbent on you to get back to your CEO with some thoughts about how you can solve that problem. I've found that CEOs really appreciate it when you come back to the table with better ideas on how to attack the issue.

Check in frequently

As a marketer, don't go dark on the CEO for extended periods of time. You never want your CEO wondering what you're up to. Make sure you are continually updating them on the progress you're making with your program. I make it a point to check in with my CEO at least once a week and do deep-dive meetings on a monthly basis.

More steak, less sizzle

When presenting to the CEO, get rid of the pretty pictures. I know that's often hard for marketers to do. We like pretty pictures. But your CEO is interested in quantifiable results. When I present to my CEO, most of my slides are charts and graphs. CEOs like data. That's what you need to be sharing.

Share the good and the bad

Your CEO does not expect you to be perfect. Share what's working and what's not with your program. Just make sure if you share what's not working, you clearly communicate what you are doing to fix it.

It's all about business impact

The most important things to share with your CEO are the marketing metrics related to business growth. You need to get past the vanity metrics. Show how your marketing program is driving more leads that are converting into pipeline for the business. Make sure the CEO understands the ROI on the marketing investments the company is making.

A few years back, I was at a trade show and my CEO was there. We ended up meeting for a drink after a long day on the expo hall floor. At that point, I'd been with the company for over a year. We'd really made a lot of progress during that time. As we got our drinks, the CEO turned to me and said, "I just want you to know, it's really impressive what you've built here. You've really got the marketing machine working." That was music to my ears.

The relationship between the CMO and the CEO can be challenging. But with the right strategy, open communication, and a focus on business impact, you can really turn your CEO into a huge fan of the marketing team.

KEY TAKEAWAYS

» Building the right team around you is critical to your success as a marketing leader.

» When building a team, you can't keep hiring the same kinds of people. It's important to bring in people who have new ideas and the ability to stretch.

» In today's competitive job market, you have to move fast during the hiring process to make sure you're able to get top talent. Moving too slow will cost you good candidates.

» Once you've assembled the team, you need to invest the time and energy to bring that team together and make sure the sum is greater than the parts. Doing an assessment like the DISC, Birkman, or Myers-Briggs is a good way to understand the different personalities on the team and how everyone can work together effectively.

» Leaders have to make sure they take the time to celebrate wins with the team. This helps the team feel valued and motivated to take on the next big project.

» To be a high-performing team, you have to create a "safe space" where people feel like they can share their ideas and feedback.

» It's critical for marketers to identify the bottlenecks that are impeding your progress in an organization and do everything you can to avoid them.

» To be a successful company, sales and marketing need to collaborate. Marketing needs to work hard to understand what the sales force needs and build programs and tools that will support them. Sales needs to help the marketing team understand what they need to be successful.

» The marketing team needs to be transparent with the CFO and finance department. Help them understand the value of what you are doing.

» The key to a successful relationship between a marketing leader and the CEO is a clear alignment on strategy, open communication, and a focus on driving business results.

PART 5:
AVOID SUCKING AT SMALL BUSINESS MARKETING

Becoming Your Own CMO

I get a lot of questions from small business owners about marketing. They don't have the budget to hire an agency or bring a full-time marketer on staff. Some of them have already spent a lot of money on advertising, only to see no results.

So what do you do if you don't have the marketing expertise for your business?

Well, the truth is you don't need big budgets for marketing. Many of the things that will drive the best results for your business are things you can probably do yourself. Don't be intimidated by marketing. A lot of it is common sense. You sell a product or service, and there are people who want to buy that product or service. Your job is:

1. Figure out how to reach those people.
2. Figure out what to say to them to get them to buy from you.
3. Once they buy from you, figure out how to keep them as a customer.

Once you break it down like that, it's not so intimidating. Marketing professionals get paid a lot of money for doing pretty basic stuff. A lot of my peers will hate me for saying that, but it's true.

So where do you start if you are a small business?

Website

Having a good website is critical for any business. That's how most people are going to find out about you. Think of it as your virtual store or office. When customers walk into your store, you want to make a good impression right away. For example, if you walk into a salon, you will usually see a nice reception desk with flowers and a receptionist smiling at you. The salon might have a plaque for "Best Salon in the City" on the wall. The area is designed to make a positive first impression on the customer. Think about your website the same way. When a potential customer gets to your website's homepage, what do you want them to see first? What do you want to tell them about your business? How can you convince them that they should do business with you?

For many small businesses, websites can be relatively simple – even just one page. Here's the important content to have on that page:

1. Name of the business and logo: The placement of this content is usually in the upper left-hand corner of the page.
2. Business contact information: This should also be very prominent. Don't make users scroll all the way to the bottom of the page to find out how to contact you. I recommend putting the contact number in the upper right-hand corner of the page.
3. Value proposition: You should have a clear and concise message about what your business does and why someone coming to the website should choose to do business with you. It is good to be as specific as possible about the kinds of customers you are serving.
4. What you offer: List out your products and services.
5. Client testimonials: Quotes from satisfied customers who have used your products and services. Show 5-star reviews that have been posted to various review sites.
6. Awards and accolades: People want to know they're making a smart choice in selecting your business. Showing the accolades you've received will give them that confidence.
7. Team members: Showing the team who runs the business is a great way to make a more human connection. It will help visitors to the website understand the people with whom they will be working.

Here's a basic 1-page template you can use when designing your business website.

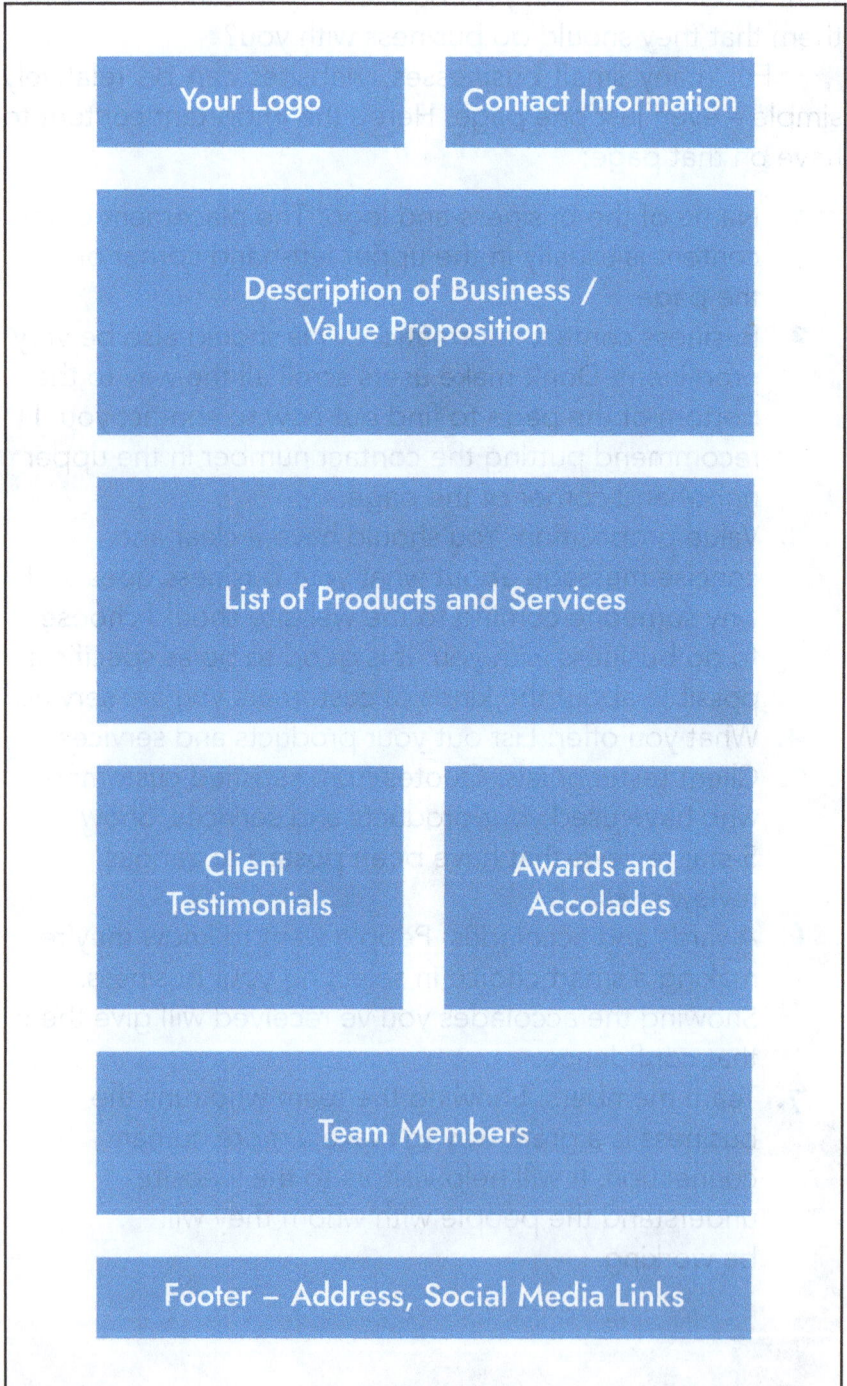

Your Logo	Contact Information

Description of Business / Value Proposition

List of Products and Services

Client Testimonials	Awards and Accolades

Team Members

Footer – Address, Social Media Links

You might be thinking, "Okay, Jeff, I understand the content I need, but how in the world do I build a website? I'm not technical."

Well, the good news is, high-quality website creation has become very easy in the past few years. There are many companies out there that give you the tools you need to build your website. It's as easy as dragging and dropping different elements on a page.

Companies like Squarespace, Wix, Weebly, and WordPress make it easy to build a professional website that looks great on desktop or mobile. They offer an extensive template library, so you can pick the style that works best for you. These companies usually offer a free option, but it's usually worth the small amount of money to upgrade to the professional version. Some of these companies also offer professional services where you can hire a person on an hourly basis to help you out.

So if you're a small business owner, don't be intimidated. There are great tools out there that make it easy to build your own website.

Google

Like it or not, Google is critical to your business. You have to make sure Google can find your website. Most of the website companies I listed above offer sites that are optimized for search engines. That means Google will most likely be able to find you as long as you have text on the website that explains who you are and what you do.

The best thing to do is search for your business on Google and see where you come up. If you're not on page one, you have a problem. So how do you fix it? First, look at your website. You have to make sure your site is built in a way that Google can read it. This is called "Search Engine Optimization," or SEO for short.

If you build your site in a tool like Squarespace, they give you an SEO checklist to help. They also offer extensive resources in their help center that tell you exactly what to do to improve your search engine ranking. If you're still struggling, you may need to hire someone to help you out. There are also plenty of online demos you can watch if you'd prefer to do it yourself.

YOUR WEBSITE AND SEARCH ENGINE PRESENCE ARE THE KEY TO ATTRACTING CONSUMERS TO YOUR PRODUCT.

Once you've fixed your SEO, it's important to look at the overall category you compete in. For example, if you own a salon in Atlanta, you should search for "best salons in Atlanta" and see what comes up. There might be online reviews or articles in the local media. Is your salon included in those lists? If not, you will want to reach out to the publishers to make sure they know about you and ask to be included on the list.

Search engine optimization can be a bit complicated and time consuming, so it might be worth investing in a consultant who can help you out.

Review Sites

When doing a Google search for your business or category, you almost always see links for the big review sites like Yelp or TripAdvisor. These sites let you create profiles for your business where your customers can leave reviews. It's very important to have a presence on these sites because they rank so high in the Google search results. Creating your business profile is a relatively straightforward process and is something you just need to do. These sites can be great for showcasing positive user reviews.

Many businesses will also incentivize their happy customers to post positive reviews. This is a best practice. If you compare two businesses on Yelp, and one has hundreds of positive reviews, and the other just has a handful of mixed reviews, you'll probably lean toward the business with more reviews when making a choice.

Make sure to address any negative reviews as soon as possible. Something will inevitably go wrong at some point, and a customer will be unhappy and vent on a review site. For a marketer, what happened to make the customer angry is not as important as how you resolve the issue. Take the time to craft a thoughtful response and ask the reviewer what you could do to make it right. If you can resolve the issue with the customer, ask them to either remove the negative review or update it to share the resolution.

People reading the negative reviews will see that you have taken the time to respond. That shows you genuinely care about your customers, and at least you're trying to provide a great experience. Just letting negative reviews sit out there unanswered could give the impression that you don't care, so make sure to stay on top of these review sites. They can help or hurt your business.

Amazon

If you're selling a product, Amazon is a necessity. You have to be there. In your product listing, make sure to provide as much detail as possible. A good exercise is to look up listings for similar products and see what they do, then build yours in a similar way. The best products on Amazon have strong written descriptions, multiple photos, videos, and extensive Q&A content. Also, reviews are very important on Amazon, so when you ship the product, make sure you have a postcard in the package that encourages or even incentivizes the buyer to post a positive review. Products with more Amazon reviews generally rank higher in the search results.

Here's one example of how you can do this:

I bought a natural shampoo on Amazon. In the packaging, there was a note offering to send me a free bottle of that same shampoo if I wrote a review and emailed them the proof. So I posted a positive review and emailed a screenshot. A few weeks later, a package showed up with a free bottle of the shampoo. It was a win-win for the company and me.

Social Media

Many small business owners are obsessed with social media. Many small business owners do nothing on social media. There's no right or wrong answer when it comes to using social media for your business.

Here's a way to think about it: If you're spending all day on social media and neglecting your business, you're going to have a problem. At the same time, if you do nothing at all on social media, you're probably missing out on some business opportunities. The trick for small businesses is finding that sweet spot where you're doing enough but not overdoing it.

Set up your business' social media accounts across all the leading platforms – Facebook, Instagram, Twitter, and LinkedIn. (Note: LinkedIn might not be necessary depending on the type of business.) There's also TikTok and Snapchat, which have large audiences, but I wouldn't focus on those channels to start. Spend time creating a nice profile with pictures, videos, and all the information about your business. Try to do one or two posts a week related to your business. Maybe you're doing a sale or have an event coming up – use your social channels to promote those activities.

I'd recommend blocking time once a week or setting a calendar reminder to do your social posts. Try out a variety of posts and see which ones get more engagement. If you have a business that lends itself well to photos, make sure you take some good ones and use the social apps' filters to make the images pop.

Again, you can also study similar businesses' social media. What are they doing well? Take those best practices and apply them to your social media channels.

I'll share a quick story to show how social media can help your business.

My wife started seeing these beautiful food photos on Instagram posted by a private chef in Atlanta. He would prepare these amazing dinners for small home parties and post a lot of photos on Instagram in the process. She became obsessed with his Instagram, and we eventually hired the chef to do a dinner at our house. Now that's a great example of how to use social media to build business and get more clients!

Chef Oh (@TheRealChefOh on Instagram) did what a lot of entrepreneurs do with social media: He used it to highlight his work and share it with current clients, who then shared it with their networks. As he catered more dinners, he organically grew his network through the networks of his clients. Over time, he's created a nice business and is booked up for months in advance.

Now, Chef Oh happens to be very good at social media. It's highly intuitive for him – he just gets it. It's not like that for everyone. But social media can be a great asset to your overall marketing program. Don't be afraid of it. Dive in and give it a try.

Email

Many consider email to be "old school," but it can be very effective, especially with your current base of customers. There's a good reason why our personal inboxes are filled with emails trying to sell us something – they work!

For small businesses, you have a lot of inexpensive options when it comes to email. Services like MailChimp enable you to build and send professional-looking emails and then track the results. You'll see who opened them, clicked, unsubscribed, and more. Building the emails is as easy as dragging and dropping images and text on a page. MailChimp was actually built for non-technical people to use.

Another benefit of MailChimp – the price! It's free for a basic plan. Even an upgraded plan with more features is only about $10 a month. It's an excellent tool for small businesses to get started with email marketing.

So what kind of emails should you send? Obviously, it will depend on your type of business, but here's a few to consider:

» Sales or discounts
» Customer satisfaction surveys
» Monthly newsletter
» Customer appreciation
» Alerts about changes to business operations
» Celebrations of accolades
» New product offerings
» Seasonal campaigns
» Appointment reminders
» Re-engaging lost customers
» Happy birthday messages to customers

Now, you don't have to do all of these, but you'll want to have a consistent cadence of emails going to your customers on a regular basis.

My wife used to run a salon in Atlanta that specialized in just blowouts. They didn't do cut or color – only wash and style. Here's an example of how she would use email. After every appointment, she would send an email asking the client to rate their satisfaction with their service. For any clients who gave low scores, my wife would personally follow up immediately to see how she could make it right. She often gave discounts or a free blowout for the next visit. As a result, she built a loyal following and was frequently named "Best Salon in Atlanta."

It's important not to think of email as just a thing to send. It's a way to engage with your customers and make sure they are satisfied with your business. It's a way to keep them coming back.

Taking It to The Next Level

To be completely honest, if you do those six things listed above reasonably well, you don't have to do much else other than run your business. Just focus on those six things. Like with social media, you can schedule time on your calendar every week to focus on marketing. Depending on how much time you can afford, you could do this once a week or once a day. Just make sure you set aside time to think about marketing on a consistent basis because without it, you will have a tough time attracting the customers to your business.

Now you might be thinking, "Okay Jeff, I've been doing those six things on a consistent basis and getting good results. What's next?" Well, once you've got the basics down, you can start to expand your marketing in other areas.

Google Search Ads

If you're doing well with SEO as I described earlier, you could try to buy some Google Search Ads. With search ads, you bid on a specific term. When a person searches for that term in Google, you will show up as an "ad" at the top of the search results. So if you own a wine store in Atlanta, you might want to bid on the term "wine store in Atlanta" to show up at the top of the page. Google gives you all the tools to easily buy search ads and monitor the results. They even make suggestions about what terms you should bid on.

It's important to note that search ads could get expensive. Because it's a bidding system, often the most popular search

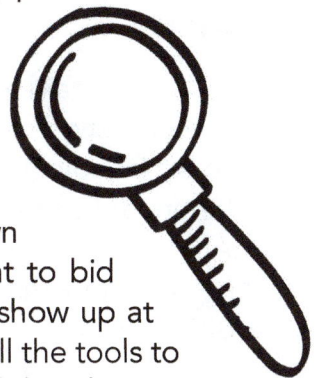

terms might be several dollars per click – but you only pay if someone does click on your ad. It's worth trying out to see if you can acquire customers at a reasonable cost. Just be aware that 70%–80% of people click on the natural search results in Google; only 20%–30% click on the paid placements. That's why you always need to focus on SEO first, paid ads second.

Facebook Ads

Social media sites also offer paid advertising options. These could be a very effective way to reach your target audience, or they could be a big waste of money. You're going to have to test and figure out what works best for your category of business.

For consumer-centric businesses, I highly recommend trying Facebook advertising. It's easy to do, and you can use very specific targeting, all the way down to a zip code and particular interests. For example, you can target people in the 30328 zip code who are parents of young kids and like wine! I would probably show up in that audience profile. The other nice thing about Facebook advertising is that you can run the same ad across Instagram (which is owned by Facebook), extending your reach.

Amazon Ads

Amazon paid ads are similar to Google, but there's a big difference between Google and Amazon ads. When you buy an ad on Google, it has no impact on where you will show up in the unpaid or natural search results. When you buy an ad on Amazon, it does have an impact. So if you want to rank higher on the Amazon search for your product, you might consider buying your way up the page.

As with any advertising investment, I strongly recommend you start small. Run some tests and see if the ads are actually working. If they are, you may want to increase your spend. If not, save that money or spend it elsewhere. It's very easy to overspend on digital advertising and not get anything for it. Take a conservative approach, figure out what works, and then dial up your spend.

Traditional Advertising

Traditional advertising like TV, radio, magazines, newspapers, and outdoor billboards are often overlooked in favor of digital. Traditional media is still relatively expensive and is not as targeted as Google or Facebook ads. Plus, it's difficult to measure the results. But in some cases, it can still be very effective. Local cable TV providers will often film a commercial for you if you agree to run it on their channels. You can then post that ad on your website and social channels. In some cities where there's bad traffic, radio can be a particularly effective medium because people spend a lot of time in their cars. If you have a retail store, buying a billboard near your location can help drive foot traffic. For certain kinds of businesses, traditional ads might be worth trying.

Direct Mail

Believe it or not, there's still a lot of opportunity in the physical mailbox. Sending targeted postcards with specific offers can be a high impact and relatively inexpensive way to get customers. The key to a successful direct mail campaign is to have a clear "call to action" (CTA) that includes an offer you can track.

Public Relations

Doing public relations (PR) can help you get articles about your business published in local media. For PR, it's often useful to engage a firm that specializes in your type of business. A good PR firm can help identify what specific publications or journalists you should target with your message. Then they will help you craft a story you can pitch.

The nice thing about PR is that it's not a paid ad, and people may be more likely to watch or read it.

Writing a Blog

Creating a blog for your business can be a nice way to engage customers and prospects with your own original content. Blog content can showcase many of the features and benefits of your business in a more expansive format. You can explain what you do and why it has value to your prospects. You can also use blog posts to highlight customer case studies, employee achievements, or your company culture. A benefit of writing a blog is that it provides more content for your website that will make it more relevant to search engines, so a good blog may get you a lot more traffic to your website.

I've had my own blog for many years. I use it as a platform to share my thoughts on advertising and marketing, and every year I usually get about 2000 to 3000 visitors to the site.

At one point in 2018, I wrote an article about my experience doing a career day presentation at my daughter's elementary school. The title of my post was "How to Crush Your Elementary School Career Day Presentation."[13] I didn't think much of the article at the time I wrote it – it was just a fun recap of my experience at the career day event. Then suddenly in 2019, about a year after I'd originally published the post, I started getting a lot of messages from random people who had read my article. I checked my website analytics and found that my traffic was way up. I wasn't sure what was going on.

Then I realized that the career day article was on page one of Google for "Career Day Presentations." I guess there are a lot of moms and dads out there looking for these tips.

---

13. If you're interested, you can see the full blog post here: https://singlemindedproposition.com/2018/07/02/how-to-crush-your-elementary-school-career-day-presentation/.

Now my blog gets ten times the traffic it did before I posted the career day article. It shows you how the right article on the right topic that gets ranked by Google can help get people to your website.

Upgrading Your Technology Stack

As you get more sophisticated with your marketing program, you might find that the tools you're using are limited. An email marketing tool like MailChimp is great, but it's designed to do the basics. If you're ready to step up your game, you may consider a tool like Hubspot that offers a lot more features and functionality – everything from email to social media management to live chat and more. The downside? It costs more. The HubSpot professional subscription currently costs around $900 a month, but for your business, it might be worth it.

Networking

One of the best strategies when trying to figure out your marketing program is to find someone who does marketing that you like and go talk to that person. You'd be surprised how people are willing to share. Now, you probably won't be able to do this with your main competitor, but there are plenty of smart marketers out there to talk to. If you get the meeting with a good marketer, just ask them how they do what they do. They may be able to recommend some good vendors you can use for your marketing program.

I'm constantly meeting with peers who want to pick my brain. It's a great way to get to know people in the community and see what they're doing. Oftentimes, I'm happy to share some of the agencies I use for my marketing program. If they want to talk to that agency, I'm always willing to make the introduction. Having a strong peer network you can tap into is always a great strategy when it comes to figuring out your marketing plan.

KEY TAKEAWAYS

» For a small business, the key when developing a marketing plan is to figure out (1) how to reach the potential buyers of your product, (2) what to say to them to get them to buy, and (3) once they buy, how to keep them as a customer.

» Having a good website is critical to your business. Think of it as your virtual store or office. There are great tools out there that make it cheap and easy to build a high-quality website.

» You need to make sure your business ranks on Google for relevant search terms. This requires search engine optimization (SEO) for your website.

» Make sure to pay attention to review sites like Yelp and TripAdvisor. If you get a lot of positive reviews, that can help your business. And remember to take the time to respond to negative reviews.

» If you're selling a product, you can't avoid Amazon. After you sell a product on Amazon, encourage the buyer to post a review. This will help you show up higher in the search results.

» For social media, focus on the leading social platforms – Facebook, Instagram, Twitter, and LinkedIn. Block off time once a week to schedule your social posts. Try out a variety of posts to see which ones get more engagement.

» Email is a great way to engage with your customers on an ongoing basis and make sure they are satisfied with your business.

» Once you get the basics right, you can move on to more advanced tactics like Google Search Ads, Facebook Ads, public relations, and more.

» One of the best strategies when trying to figure out your marketing program is networking. Find someone who does marketing you like and go talk to them.

PART 6:
CRISIS DOES SUCK,
BUT YOU CAN THRIVE

Marketing in the Time of COVID

I wrote the majority of this book in 2020 while the entire country was shut down because of the COVID-19 pandemic. It was definitely a tough year. I worked from home after we closed our office in March. I won't lie, it was a challenge for me. I've spent 20+ years working in an office environment. I'm definitely an "office creature." I like wandering the halls, having conversations, and doing drive-bys to brainstorm ideas. I guess it's hard to teach an old dog new tricks. But like everyone else, I adapted. I spent a lot of my day on Zoom calls with my team and other groups in the company. And we were very productive during COVID. I think we actually got more done in 2020 than my previous two years at the company. Nevertheless, now that people are being vaccinated and you can see the light at the end of the tunnel, I really look forward to being back in the office, collaborating face-to-face.

COVID had a significant impact on ParkMobile. We help people pay for parking on their mobile device. And if people were not going out, they were not parking. I will say that January and February 2020 were great months for ParkMobile. We were literally breaking records every week.

We have a Slack channel where we track the daily metrics, and you'd frequently see messages posted by our data team saying things like "Best Monday in company history," "another record-breaking week," "We're up 50% versus last year." Every Slack message was cheered by employees with a barrage of "atta-boys" and celebratory emojis. It seemed like the success would never end. Until it did.

In early March 2020, the warning signs around COVID started to intensify. You'd see people wearing masks in the grocery store. Then in the second week of March, it was like a bomb dropped. In one day, the NCAA canceled the March Madness basketball tournament, Tom Hanks announced he had COVID, and the President gave an Oval Office address about it. Suddenly, it was all too real. Schools went virtual. Offices closed. States issued stay-at-home orders. We saw our booming business fall off a cliff – down 95% overnight!

Those were some dark days back in March and April. The pandemic was a crisis for the country and a crisis for our business. We had about 200 employees all wondering if they would have a job in a month. None of us had experienced anything like this before. We were in uncharted territory, but we had to start making decisions to weather the storm.

The Show Must Go On

A crisis is a real test for a marketing leader. Since marketing usually controls a large variable budget, it will always be a big target for the CEO and CFO when trying to reduce expenses.

So what do you do?

Let's start with what you don't do

» You don't put your head in the sand and pretend it's business as usual.
» You don't try to hold on to your marketing budget at all costs.

» You don't fall back on conventional wisdom like "we have to always be on" or "a downturn is when you need to invest more in marketing."

» You don't just focus on your marketing silo, rather than taking a broad look at the entire organization.

This is the kind of thinking that will get you fired pretty quickly during a crisis.

Like every other leader in the company dealing with the crisis, you have to make some tough decisions. Because if you're not willing or able to make those decisions, guess who will make them for you? Your CEO and CFO. And that won't be pretty.

Your Key Leadership Crisis Actions

Make significant budget cuts

As I said before, marketing usually has a lot of variable budget. Take a magnifying glass to each item and ask yourself the tough questions. Do you really need to spend this money right now? Would this money be better allocated to other parts of the company? It's never fun to cut your own budget, but during a crisis you have no choice. And if you don't do it yourself, expect your CFO to just take an ax to it. It's better that you control where to make the cuts.

Renegotiate your vendor contracts

During a crisis, your vendors may provide some flexibility to strengthen the relationship for the long term. Some may let you out of a contract, reduce your cost, or provide favorable payment terms. It's essential that you look at each vendor and see what your options are. For me, the vendors that were more flexible during COVID really strengthened our relationship, ensuring that I'll be back doing business with them in a post-COVID world.

Reallocate underutilized personnel

Inevitably, if you are shutting down parts of your marketing program, you may have staff without things to do. For example, all our in-person trade shows and events were canceled for 2020. We had a dedicated person on the team who managed these events since it was a pretty busy job, with over 50 national and regional events every year. Without those events, our employee had very little to do. We found a few new projects for her to take on, but we realized we didn't need that resource on our team right now. At the same time, our operations team needed some additional help. We gave our employee an opportunity to stay with the company in a different role that would be better utilized at the current time, creating a win-win for the employee and the company.

Rethink your overall marketing program

Winston Churchill once said, "Never let a good crisis go to waste." For better or worse, one thing COVID did is force us to rethink everything. This presents a big opportunity for marketers to really question their program. What's working? What's not? For ParkMobile, we found several things we were doing that didn't seem to be making much of an impact on the business. In a normal world, you fall back on the "we've always done it that way" mindset. COVID forced us to ask the tough questions about our program. As a result, we've been much more focused on the things that actually drive the business, and we've gotten rid of a lot of the noise.

The points above are really applicable to any crisis, not just COVID. In fact, I could have probably written something similar during the financial crisis in 2008 or the dotcom bust in the early 2000s. So let me be more specific and tell you about some of the things we did during COVID.

Increase messaging relevance

COVID created an opportunity to evolve our messaging to be more relevant to the times. ParkMobile has always focused on being a "smarter way to park." That's a fairly broad statement and probably means different things to different people. It plays on the insight that the old way of paying for parking – at a meter or paying an attendant – is pretty dumb. Paying for parking with an app is smart.

During COVID, we saw a bigger insight related to the term "contactless." Cities and businesses were all talking about going contactless to prevent the spread of the virus. This played perfectly for our business. Do you really want to touch a meter or hand cash to an attendant when you can make a contactless parking payment? The answer is no!

We quickly shifted our messaging to focus on "contactless parking payments." We found this resonated with both our users and many of our city clients. As we started aggressively promoting contactless parking to the industry, we found that we increased our sales team's lead volume. In a challenging year for our business, we signed more new clients than ever before.

Stay relevant and provide support

What do you do when people no longer need your product? How do you stay relevant? As people stopped going out, they stopped parking, so they no longer needed the ParkMobile app. I saw many social posts about how people were deleting the app from their phone because they no longer needed it.

We asked ourselves, how can we keep people using the app, even if they aren't parking? Our team came up with the idea of converting the app into a charitable giving tool, providing donations to communities affected by COVID. With your ParkMobile account, you could quickly and easily donate to a local or national charity. We even matched a portion of the donations, raising over $36,000 in a short amount of time.

This program was a great way to keep our brand top of mind and build more loyalty by doing some good for the community.

Increase civic engagement

As cities started to reopen, leaders wanted to make sure people were safe while they were out and about. We partnered with many of our clients to promote safety protocols to our large user base in the local area. Leveraging our digital engagement tools, we did a series of emails and in-app messages to encourage social distancing, mask wearing, and frequent hand washing.

That worked particularly well for the state of Delaware. They saw many people were heading to the Delaware beaches that summer, and they wanted to make sure people were safe. We partnered with the Governor's communications team on a "Summer Safely" campaign, targeting almost 1,000,000 people across the state.

The campaign worked so well that Delaware Governor Jay Carney even gave us a shoutout on social media! That's not something that happens every day.

Give away expertise to the industry

ParkMobile's challenges were not isolated to just our company. The entire parking industry was feeling the pain. From cities losing out on critical parking revenue to garage operators who had to make drastic staff reductions, the pandemic had broad impacts for every parking organization.

To support the industry, ParkMobile leveraged our audience and data to provide critical insights to our clients. We released several reports that tracked current and projected trends related to parking. We conducted an extensive research study on how COVID will change consumer behavior and shared those results with the industry. Additionally, we looked across our clients to see the best practices that were emerging during the pandemic. Then we shared those best practices with our base of clients, providing ideas that they could implement in their city or operation. Providing this valuable content helped strengthen our relationships with our clients during this difficult time.

Patch the Leaky Bucket

As marketing budgets were significantly reduced, our team had to refocus our efforts. During normal times, most of our resources are directed to user acquisition. We want to grow our audience of users at a rapid pace. The more users of the app, the more revenue we can generate.

Without the budgets to invest in digital advertising and other programs, we shifted our focus from acquisition to retention. We asked ourselves: where are we losing users and where are we missing out on conversions?

What we found was that we had a leaky bucket problem. We were really good at filling up the bucket and acquiring users, but we were letting a lot of those users leak out after they initially registered for the app.

So we refocused all of our attention on retaining those users and getting them to transact more often. The good thing here was that we'd already acquired the user, so we didn't need money to retain them. We just needed to find new ways to make sure we kept them engaged over time, so they would continue using the app whenever and wherever they parked.

Our team looked for the key trigger points where a user would become inactive. One area was related to adding a payment method in the app. We would see many users download ParkMobile and set up their account, but they wouldn't add a payment method. The majority of those people would never initiate a transaction.

Now, why didn't they add a payment method? Well, maybe they didn't have their wallet with them at the time. Perhaps they got distracted during the setup process and never came back to the app. Whatever the reason, we saw an opportunity to remind people to add that payment method. Once we implemented this campaign, we saw an immediate bump in our conversions from those users.

Another trigger point we saw was when a credit card would expire in the app. We've probably all experienced this in the past. You go to pay for something online, and the card on file is expired. It's pretty inconvenient.

So if you're parking with the app and this happens, you may just opt to use the meter rather than update your credit card on file. It might be quicker. Again, that's a lost user for ParkMobile.

Our team started a campaign that would proactively alert users who had a credit card on file if it was about to expire. We notify them through emails and in-app messages and encourage them to update it in the app. As we ran this campaign, we saw thousands of people update their card on file. This ensures those people can continue to pay with the app and fixes another leak in the bucket.

In any marketing program, you will have trigger points where you lose customers or prospects. The key is to identify what those points are and put programs in place to prevent that loss – in other words, patch the leaky bucket.

The Comeback

As I'm writing this book, our business has made a significant comeback from those dark days back in March and April 2020. We're starting to see a return to year-over-year growth once again, which is really nice. We know we're not out of the woods yet, but it's good to see we're making progress.

We've learned some valuable lessons during this time that will serve us very well once we're on the other side. Until then, we will remain focused on keeping our marketing expenses low while maximizing our impact on the business.

KEY TAKEAWAYS

» When there is a crisis for the business, marketing leaders have to be very proactive in trying to reduce expenses to help the company weather the storm.

» Closely analyze your budget and find the places where you can cut costs. If you aren't willing to make the tough decisions, your CEO and CFO will make them for you.

» Reach out to your vendors and see if there are options to renegotiate or pause contracts. Good partners will understand the situation and try to help as much as possible.

» Look for opportunities to reallocate underutilized staff to other departments. That's a better option than letting people go.

» Don't let a good crisis go to waste. Take the opportunity to rethink your entire marketing program from top to bottom.

» A crisis may create opportunities to increase the relevance of your brand messaging. For example, during COVID, ParkMobile shifted its message to focus on "contactless payments," which was very relevant during the pandemic.

» During tough times, look for opportunities to support the community as much as you can. This will keep your brand top of mind and build loyalty.

» Providing data and insights to your clients during a crisis is a good way to build stronger relationships.

» If your marketing budget gets cut during a crisis, look for other ways to improve results that do not require financial investments. Specifically, if you don't have the budget to acquire new customers, think about what you can do to better retain your current base of customers.

PART 7: MARKETING LESSONS AS MEMOIR

My Career

Young marketing professionals often ask me about my career journey. I think there's a mindset that if you want to be a CMO someday, there's a certain "path" you need to take. Well, my journey has not been very conventional. There was no "master plan." I didn't work my way up through the ranks of one company or have a clearly defined path to the C-suite. Rather, my journey has been a long exercise in trial and error. I've had a lot of marketing jobs. And in every position, I've learned that there are things I like to do and things I really don't like to do. Every time I move to a new opportunity, I try to find a position that has more of the stuff I like and less of the stuff I don't like. It's really that simple.

In this section, I'll share my professional journey from college to CMO. You'll see how every job was a learning opportunity that helped me figure out where I eventually wanted to be.

Unfocused Beginnings

I really never knew what I wanted to be when I grew up. As I entered my junior and senior years of high school, I was just clueless. If it wasn't about girls or basketball, I wasn't interested. I went through the motions of taking the SAT and applying to college, but I didn't know what I wanted to do or where I wanted to go. I think I applied to about 20 different schools, which shows how unfocused I was at the time.

I guess I always liked studying history and government, so I thought that might lead to a career in politics. I was also VP of the student government, so I liked the idea of potentially being a mayor, congressman, or governor, but I had no idea what that involved.

This interest in government and politics led me to American University in Washington, DC. I mean, if you want to work in government, what better place to be? And it was a good four years that included some great internship opportunities at the White House, the Equal Employment Opportunity Commission (EEOC), and the Department of Health and Human Services. I took classes with some outstanding professors, including Julian Bond, a civil rights leader and former head of the NAACP; Van Dorn Ooms, former Capitol Hill economist; and James Thurber, a noted political scholar.

At the end of my four years at American, I still didn't have a clue what I wanted to do. While a job in politics seemed like the natural path, I could not find many opportunities upon graduation. I remember interviewing with a few political campaigns that wanted me to work for free. After funding four years of private school education, I didn't want to tell my parents I was going to take an unpaid gig.

Also, when it came right down to it, I didn't like the idea of working in politics. After all the internships and coursework, I think I realized it just wasn't for me. Some people go to college and learn what they want to do. I guess at least I learned what I didn't want to do.

So there I was, in my last few weeks at school without a clue what I was going to do after graduation. Fortunately for me, I had an uncle who had spent his career in marketing and executive positions at Johnson & Johnson. He sent my resume around to some of the New York ad agencies he worked with and helped me get a foot in the door. These agencies were all happy to talk to the nephew of one of their most important clients.

Now, I didn't take any business courses at American. I had no clue what an ad agency did. But I did take a lot of classes on political communication. In my senior year, my capstone project was developing a complete political ad campaign for one of the presidential candidates. I had a portfolio of political ads that I packaged up and brought with me to my interviews. I'm sure the interviewers at the ad agencies were highly amused when I walked in with my "Bob Dole for President" storyboards. The reality is, they were doing a favor for an important client and gave me my first break.

I accepted a position at Saatchi & Saatchi as an Assistant Account Executive with a salary of $24,000 a year. I was on my way to New York City to start my career in advertising.

Key Career Lesson: Sometimes it's just as important to figure out what you *don't* want to do in your career as it is to figure out what you really want to do.

Hello, Saatchi & Saatchi

I arrived at the Saatchi & Saatchi office at the corner of Hudson and Houston in Soho in August of 1996. As a newcomer to New York City, I didn't appreciate how hot and muggy it would be in the summer. Wanting to make a good impression on my first day, I wore my best blazer, which happened to be made of a very heavy, non-breathable wool. I walked several blocks from my apartment in Murray Hill to the subway and took the train down to Soho, then walked several more blocks to get to the office.

By the time I got there, I was absolutely soaked with sweat. It was seeping through my undershirt to my dress shirt. I had to spend about 15 minutes in the bathroom drying myself off before I went in for my HR orientation. But it didn't do any good. I was going to walk into the first day of my first job a sweaty mess. There was nothing I could do about it.

They took all the new hires to a conference room for orientation. As I looked around the room, I was impressed by the other people. They all seemed so cool and stylish. They had all gone to excellent schools, and many had done several advertising internships before joining Saatchi – exactly what you would expect at a top New York ad agency. Me, on the other hand? Well, it wasn't so pretty. My clothes were too baggy. I was losing my hair. Nothing about me at that time was "cool." I just didn't look the part.

We were given our assignments. My job would be working in a part of the agency called the "Kid Connection." We worked on the General Mills snack and cereal products that were targeted to kids, like Fruit Roll-Ups, Gushers, and Dunkaroos.

I spent my first day at Saatchi getting acclimated, meeting the team, and setting up my workspace. Around 5:30 pm, I packed up my bag and headed home. As I got in the elevator, Jennifer Kahn, another new hire from orientation, was in the elevator holding a large stack of videotapes. I said hi and asked how her first day was. She said it was great. Then she looked at me with my bag on my shoulder and said, "You're leaving already?" The elevator door opened, and she stepped out, saying with a tinge of sarcasm, "Have a great night."

I guess it wasn't the best first day. But it would get a lot better.

I quickly got into the flow working at Saatchi. It was an entry-level job. Very tactical. I would probably spend half the day running up and down the stairs between my desk and the AV room where the team would make video tape duplicates, or "dubs" as we called them.

Yeah, it was a different time. We didn't have digital video files we could email to a client. We had to make physical videotapes to ship out. After we had the tapes, we would have to watch each one to make sure they were correct and that there were no video issues.

I remember one time Julie Halpin, the General Manager of the Kid Connection, was going to a big meeting in Europe. She asked me to put a reel together with a lot of different spots the team had done over the past two years. Europe had a different kind of video format called "PAL." I took all my master videos down to the AV room, and the engineers spliced together a reel for Julie in PAL format.

We didn't have a PAL machine in the office, so there was no way for me to check to make sure the video was right. The engineers assured me it was fine, so I gave it to Julie to take on her trip. Julie called me the next day from Europe. The tape didn't work. Oh shit.

She lit into me. "Did you check the tape?" she yelled over the phone.

"Um, well, it's PAL, and we don't have a PAL machine," I said. "So I couldn't check it."

I don't remember the entire conversation from that point on, but it wasn't pretty. And she was totally in the right. I screwed up and put her in a horrible position at a big client meeting. It was an important lesson for me in attention to detail.

I felt terrible. I ran down to the engineers to tell them what happened. We put together another tape. This time I had to stand over the engineer's shoulder to watch it back to ensure the conversion to the PAL format was correct. I ended up watching it back multiple times just to make sure it was right. Then I ran to FedEx and shipped it overnight to Europe.

When Julie got back from her trip, I wasn't sure what to expect. Maybe I would get fired. Or at least get another dressing down over the mistake. Fortunately for me, she never mentioned it again. She quickly moved on, and so did I. But I always felt terrible about that. I wanted to say something to Julie but never had the nerve. So, Julie Halpin, if you happen to be reading this book, I sincerely apologize for not checking the tape and putting you in that position.

I spent a lot of hours at the agency. Not always because I had to be there, but if you stayed at work after 7:30 pm, the company would pay for your cab home and give you $10 towards dinner. That worked for me and a lot of my fellow account managers as well. We weren't well paid, so we spent extra time at the office for a free ride home and a cheap meal. When you are living in an expensive city like New York, every little bit helps.

Plus, I didn't have a family to go home to, and the dumpy one-bedroom apartment I shared wasn't a great place to spend a lot of time. So I just hung out around the Saatchi office. There was always a crew of us who would be there late. Eventually, we all became friends and started spending a lot of time at the bars near the office. Every Friday, there would be a gaggle of us leaving the office around 6 pm to get drinks. Many times, I wouldn't get home until early the next morning.

Jenn Kahn, the girl who had shamed me on my first day for leaving early, became one of my best friends at work – my first "work wife." She lived with her boyfriend, who was in law school, so she didn't see him much. We spent a lot of time hanging out after work with a crew of junior-level Saatchi employees.

Those were fun times. We worked hard and played hard. I learned early on that there were many media sales reps in NYC who desperately wanted to work with the Saatchi clients. There were constant offers of fancy lunches, dinners, VIP parties, and even a sunset cruise on the Forbes yacht! And I was always happy to accept an invite.

So, while I was making less than $40,000 a year in NYC, I was dining out at the finest restaurants and landing on the VIP lists at the hottest clubs. It didn't seem quite right. But I wasn't going to complain. I was living a pretty good lifestyle on my meager account executive salary.

One thing I'll never forget about working at Saatchi were the epic holiday parties. They were legendary. The company would always rent out some swanky venue, and it would just be pure debauchery. It wasn't uncommon to see C-level executives (who were married) making out on the dance floor with junior associates. At least at those parties, Madison Avenue lived up to its reputation.

The parties were always on a weeknight, so I remember showing up the next day to a mostly empty office as everyone called in sick to nurse their hangover. The people who did show up spent most of the day gossiping about who hooked up or who made a fool of themselves at the party.

I was lucky at Saatchi & Saatchi to have a great first boss, a guy named Marc Greengrass. Marc also started as an assistant account executive and had been in the business for a few years. He took me under his wing and showed me the ropes. Even though he was swamped, he always took the time to explain all the details to me and coach me on how things worked at the agency.

I spent most of my days shadowing Marc, and he gave me a template for how to operate at the agency. I think the biggest thing I learned from him early on was the importance of following up. After any client meeting, Marc would write up a detailed conference report and send it to all attendees. Then he would consistently track all the commitments written down in the conference report until we had the next client meeting.

With Marc leading the account, nothing ever slipped through the cracks. And the client really appreciated that. They knew they could count on us. We never got into an awkward exchange in meetings about "well, I thought we said this" or "you told me this last time." It was all well documented in the conference report and agreed to.

I remember one contentious meeting when the client didn't think we had made the requested edits to a print ad. Marc pulled out the conference report and read precisely what the client agreed to in the previous meeting. It was great to see him back the client down merely by repeating his words back to him.

By following Marc's lead, I learned the three critical skills necessary to make it through those early career years:

1. Show that you are willing to work hard
2. Pay attention to the smallest details
3. Demonstrate that the team can depend on you every step of the way

After about a year, those lessons helped me get promoted to account executive and transferred to the Procter & Gamble team, working on the Tide laundry detergent account. While I was sad to leave Marc, this was an opportunity to continue to grow my career with one of the most high-profile clients in the agency.

After the fruit snack category, I wasn't sure if I would like working on a laundry detergent brand. As a 20-something single guy living in NYC without a washer or dryer in my apartment, I didn't really understand the target audience.

But on the Procter & Gamble account, you didn't have to be a heavy user of the product as long as you were willing to put in the work to learn about the consumer. The great thing about working on the Tide account was having access to all the market research, qualitative and quantitative. And I dove right in. I knew more about Tide's buyers – suburban moms with 2.5 kids – than I did about most other subjects. I could spend hours talking about the insights related to laundry and how the act of doing laundry for the family is really an extension of how parents nurture their kids.

I remember sitting behind the double-sided mirror in a focus group and listening to a group of eight moms talking about doing laundry for their family. It was amazing to see this focus group turn into a support group. Once you witness a group of moms crying about laundry, you realize that a brand like Tide plays a much bigger role than one might think.

When I look back at that Tide team, I consider myself lucky to have been a part of it. It was truly a great group of people to work with. During that time, we launched the first new brand campaign for Tide in ten years. And the work I was doing made an impact. In the years I was on Tide, we saw what had been a flat market share for several years start to grow. Our work even received the coveted Effie award, given to ad campaigns that make a measurable impact on the business.

Getting to work on Tide was one of the best things that ever happened to me in my career, and the lessons I learned I still apply to my job every single day.

> **Key Career Lesson:** When you're first starting your career, you need to demonstrate that you're willing to work hard, pay attention to detail, and be dependable.

5 Key Lessons Learned from Proctor & Gamble

Lesson 1: Everything starts and ends with the consumer

P&G is known for having an obsessive focus on the consumer. They had a very large in-house research team that focused on insights. Rarely would you ever hear a P&G brand manager say, "I think…" More likely, that brand manager would say, "The consumer thinks…" There were many times my clients personally wouldn't like a specific campaign we presented but would approve it because research showed that consumers liked it. It's that discipline that has helped P&G continue to grow market share in mature categories. They build products and produce advertising that they know consumers will like. In today's fast-paced business environment, research and testing sometimes seem like a lost art. But if your business is struggling and you want to understand why, nothing compares to doing a focus group and hearing directly from customers what the issues are.

Lesson 2: You need to keep up with changing times

P&G makes products for families – laundry detergent, diapers, paper towels, dishwashing detergent, etc. If you look at old P&G ads from the '50s and '60s, they all look the same. There's a mom in the kitchen or laundry room, a dad on the couch, and the kids are outside rolling in the grass. The family is always white. But today the definition of "family" has changed. Divorce, adoption, interracial marriage, and gay marriage have redefined how we think about the stereotypical family. P&G has changed with the times as well. When I worked on the Tide brand in the mid-90s, we did TV spots about a divorced dad taking care of his kids on the weekend and a white family adopting an Asian child. These spots showed that P&G understood the modern family dynamic.

Lesson 3: Be single-minded

P&G would develop great products with a ton of great features and benefits. But when it came to advertising, they were always cautious about cramming too many features into an ad. The focus was on being single-minded with the communication. That's a lesson that has stuck with me – I even named my blog The Single Minded Proposition. I have great respect for the discipline it takes to be single-minded in your communication.

Lesson 4: Stay ahead of the curve

People would probably be surprised to hear someone call P&G an "innovative" company. I mean, how innovative can you really be with soap and diapers? But the reality is that P&G is very innovative. They closely study consumer behavior and trends. They're constantly market testing new ideas for their products. They were the first consumer packaged goods company to embrace the internet as a marketing tool. Back in the mid-90s, I worked on the original Tide.com that featured an app called the "Stain Detective."[14] It would show you how to get any stain out of any fabric. There were thousands of different combinations. There was nothing like it on the internet at the time, and it ended up getting a lot of buzz and winning awards.

---

14. If you want to check out the old Tide website, visit: web.archive.org/web/19961226195629/http://www.tide.com/.

Lesson 5: Be nice

The thing I most remember about working with P&G was that the people there were super nice. Maybe it's that midwestern Cincinnati style. Perhaps the company is just good at hiring really smart people who happen to be pleasant to work with. Whatever it is, they were always a great client that treated me well and taught me a lot about advertising early in my career. For that, I'll always be grateful. And for those who don't think P&G does good advertising, just watch some of their recent Super Bowl spots. They will probably change your mind.

The MBA: An Opportunity to Learn How Not to Suck

While I was enjoying my time in advertising, I started thinking about what was next. Did I want to be at an agency for my whole career? Or did I want to do something different? I was finding more and more that I enjoyed learning about my clients' businesses. I spent a lot of time talking with the brand managers at P&G about the strategies beyond just the ad campaigns.

During one trip to Cincinnati to meet with P&G, I was having dinner with some of our clients. One of them asked me if I planned to stay in advertising for my career. I said I wasn't sure. I liked advertising, but I also had the desire to do more. I just didn't know what "more" was.

The client suggested that if I ever wanted to move to the client side, it would serve me well to go back to school and get my MBA. All the brand managers at P&G had their MBAs from top-tier business schools – Wharton, Northwestern, Harvard, etc. This got me thinking. I never took any business classes when I was at American University. Earning an MBA could help fill some of my knowledge gaps. Plus, after working in the NYC grind for four years, the idea of going back to school was very appealing.

I started the application process and the GMAT prep. That turned out to be like a second full-time job. It's amazing how many different essays you have to write as part of your business school application. I found the quantitative section of the GMAT particularly challenging. Studying political science as an undergrad, I didn't have to take any math classes except the one required course my freshman year. That means it had been about eight years since I did any kind of math class.

I spent most weekends taking practice tests and trying to get my scores to a level where I would have a shot to get into a top-tier school. I ended up taking the formal test three times. The first time, I didn't get the score I wanted. The second time, I got a better score that put me at the lower part of the range where I needed to be.

I decided to give it one more shot. I spent about four weeks really focused on the GMAT, constantly taking practice tests, even at work. The day I went to the test center, I felt ready to go. In a room full of people taking different standardized tests, I was cruising through the quantitative section. In the GMAT, as you get more questions right, the questions get more challenging. As I saw harder questions coming up, I figured that was a good sign. I thought to myself, you are crushing this test!

I finished the math section with time to spare. I felt great. After I finished the verbal section and completed the test, a screen popped up, asking if I wanted my score. This is the point where you can cancel your GMAT score if you think you did poorly. So if you're having a bad day or you realize you made some critical errors, you have the option just to void your score for that test so you can try again another time.

But I felt like this would be the score I needed. I clicked the button, excited to see how many points my score had increased.

And there it was. The EXACT same score I had gotten the last time.

"SHIT!" I yelled out.

Everyone in the room turned and looked at me. The testing center employee shushed me, and I apologized and left.

Well, I didn't get the score I wanted, and I was done taking this test. I was going to let it ride with the score I had. I knew the schools in the top fifteen would be a reach, but with my work experience and undergrad grades, I had a shot at getting into a top-25 school.

I ended up getting into Vanderbilt, the University of Southern California, and Penn State. I was waitlisted at Emory. Of the four schools, Emory was my preference because I had some cousins in Atlanta, making it an easier transition to a new city. Vanderbilt was my second choice; they had a strong digital marketing curriculum I was very interested in. So it looked like I was headed to Nashville.

As I was finishing up my time in New York City, I was still single and active on the dating scene. One night, I went out with a girl who had just moved to the city after finishing her MBA at Emory. At some point during the date, I told her that I was on the waitlist there.

We had a great date. She was smart and fun. The conversation came very easily. We made a plan to see each other again. At the end of the night, before we went our separate ways, she said, "You know, Emory should really take you. I'm going to call them tomorrow and put in a good word."

The next day, I got a phone call from a number with a 404 area code. That's Atlanta. It was Julie Barefoot, the Dean of Admissions for Emory's business school.

"Jeff, I just got the most wonderful call from Abby Spatz," said Julie. "We take our alumni endorsements very seriously at Emory. Given that, I want to offer you a spot in the class of 2003."

Just wow. After all the work on the applications and the GMAT, who knew a random date would lead to me getting into business school? It's funny how the world works sometimes.

I thanked Julie and told her that "I accept." I was heading to Atlanta for business school.

In the summer of 2001, I loaded a U-haul truck, left New York City, and headed down to Emory University to start the MBA program. I rented an apartment in the Post Briarcliff complex, about two miles from campus. After living in tiny NYC apartments for five years, living in Atlanta was amazing. I had my own one-bedroom apartment in a nice complex with a pool and gym. And it was about a quarter of the price of my last apartment in New York.

The day after I moved in, I went down to the pool at the complex, and there was a huge party with a DJ. It was like a college spring break in Cancun. Absolutely crazy. Where was I?

At the party, I met a lot of the other incoming MBA students. Many had also just relocated from NYC, so we immediately bonded. After five years in the NYC ad industry, suddenly I felt totally free. I was turning the page and starting a new chapter! I felt great about my decision to go to Emory, and I knew it was going to be a great two years.

The first semester of business school is really hard. The volume of work and complexity of the subject matter is a challenge, even for the best students. For people who have been working full-time jobs for the past few years, the transition back into an academic setting can be a bit bumpy.

The first month I was in a constant state of stress, continually questioning my class prep and hoping I didn't get "cold called" to share my thoughts on the latest case study. In addition to the academics, from the second we walked in the door of the business school, we had to start looking for a job.

I just left a job to go to school, I thought. Now I have to start my post-MBA job search two years before I graduate? There's a good reason MBA programs put so much focus on the job search. A big metric that schools are ranked on is the post-MBA job placement. Top-tier schools like Emory are expected to place at least 90% of students with high paying MBA-caliber jobs by graduation.

So in addition to a full-time course load, students are in a constant state of job search in the first semester. So much for taking the time to figure out what you really want to do. Immediately there's a steady stream of companies coming to campus for recruiting, and I was competing with over 100 marketing MBA students for just a few interview slots.

Fortunately, I secured my MBA internship early on. I would be heading up to Philadelphia to work at GlaxoSmithKline during the summer. Once that was locked down, it removed a huge burden from my shoulders. At the time, it didn't really cross my mind whether or not the internship was the right fit for me. It was all about just landing the gig – you figure out the other stuff later.

Should I get an MBA?

I get this question from a lot of young professionals, and unfortunately, there's no right answer.

When considering going back to school for your graduate degree, you have to weigh a lot of trade-offs. The biggest risk is walking away from two years of a full-time salary and benefits. Since most MBA students have about five years of professional experience, some people could be walking away from significant income.

You also have to think about your current career path. Are you on a good track at work? Do you see a route to move up in the company? Going back to school for a full-time MBA will most likely derail your path at your current job. Most MBA students don't go back to the company or job they had before they started the program. If you want to stay with your current company, you might consider an evening or executive MBA program, which would allow you to get the degree on nights and weekends without leaving your current job.

On the other hand, if you are thinking about a career change, the MBA could be a good pivot point for you. For example, you're in accounting and want to get into marketing. You'll probably have an easier time landing that marketing gig coming out of an MBA program than you would if you tried to make the transition in the normal job market.

Just remember there's no guarantee that the MBA means you'll get a job at graduation. The fact is a lot of people graduate from top-tier MBA programs every year without a job. Depending on the school, that number can be 15% to 30% of graduates – a pretty scary prospect after spending six figures on the degree.

On the positive side, you will learn a lot. Most top-tier MBA programs have excellent faculty and innovative curriculum that will keep even the smartest minds challenged. Plus, you'll be surrounded by a lot of highly talented people who will form your professional network in the future.

Then there are the less quantitative metrics on the value of the MBA program – the friendships you make and the memories you have. In my two years at Emory, I met my future wife, Paige, and made some of my best friends, three of whom were in my wedding party. I also took amazing school trips to Brazil, Thailand, Vietnam, and Singapore.

So for me, I think getting the MBA worked out pretty well.

Key Career Lesson: Getting an MBA can help your career and be a great experience. But there are no guarantees you will get the job you want coming out of school. You need to go into the experience with your eyes wide open.

Post-MBA Career

I graduated with an MBA into a pretty uncertain future. The economy still hadn't rebounded from the dotcom bust. There were hardly any companies coming to campus to recruit. My classmates were all taking unconventional approaches to the post-MBA job search. Many of us were reaching out to our previous employers to see if there were opportunities to come back. We were looking at positions that weren't your traditional MBA jobs.

One of my professors, Charlie Goetz, introduced me to a friend of his who was working on a startup business printing college logos on floormats. Definitely not your typical MBA job. But at the time, I didn't have a lot of other options. Plus, the idea of getting in on the ground floor of a business seemed like a good opportunity. I was in a sales role, and I would make a commission based on my output. Plus, I could stay in Atlanta while my girlfriend, Paige, was finishing her second year at Emory.

I took the job. At the time, I felt lucky; many of my classmates graduated without jobs. I got my degree and was ready to embark on my post-MBA career.

The job with the floor mat company was pretty fun at first, minus the daily commute to Suwanee, Georgia, where the office was located. It was about 90 minutes of driving every day – that's a lot of time to spend in the car! But I was able to figure out some creative ways to sell a lot of these floor mats. College sports fans love their teams.

But I knew this wasn't the job for me. The longer I did it, the longer I put off finding the right job. I needed to make a change.

I thought long and hard about what I wanted to do in my career. I had enjoyed my time working in advertising and felt that it could be a good place for me to land post-MBA. I was on a great track when I left the industry, and now I had all these new skills I could apply to the job. I wasn't sure I wanted to spend the rest of my career in an agency, but it seemed like a much better jumping-off point than this floor mat company. Plus, I had a pretty good network from my agency days I could tap into to help me land a gig.

So I quit my job at the floor mat company and moved back to NYC to continue my career in advertising. It ended up being much harder to get that job (you'll remember the story back in **"The Low Point: What Happens When Your Career Hits Rock Bottom and How to Turn It Around" on page 75**), but I eventually found a gig and restarted my career in NYC.

> **Key Career Lesson:** You need to find a job that's right for you. If you don't think you're in the right role, you should consider making a change.

NYC to OMD to GSK

Having landed a job in NYC, I rented an apartment in Chelsea and moved back to the city. After being out of work and living with my parents for several months, it felt great to be back on my feet again.

My new job was with the global media planning and buying company OMD, part of Omnicom Group. I was in a department called "OMD Ignition," and our mission was to bring more strategic and creative thinking to the media buying process. Instead of just doing the same kinds of media buys year after year, we were supposed to push the teams to think differently.

This ended up being a pretty big challenge both internally and with clients. I was assigned to work on Pepsi, HBO, and Office Depot. These accounts all had well-established teams who knew what they were doing. Then I got inserted into the process to "shake things up." No one really wanted me there, and after a while, I realized things weren't going in the right direction.

Fortunately, it always seems easier to get a job when you have a job. Even though I hadn't been at OMD very long, I had many recruiters reaching out to see if I was interested in new opportunities. I didn't think it would hurt to at least go on a few interviews to see if I could find a better fit.

I ended up getting an offer to work at Euro RSCG (now called Havas) as an account director on the GlaxoSmithKline account. That's right, back to working on GSK, where I had interned as an MBA student. But this time, I'd be on the agency side. Funny how the world works.

It turned out that Euro RSCG was a much better fit for me. We had a great team at the agency and great clients to work with. I also had the opportunity to work on some new business pitches, which was fun.

> **Key Career Lesson:** It's always easier to get a job when you have a job.

The Super Bowl Ad that Got Away

People often ask me about my experience working in the ad industry. For an outsider, there seems to be a great mystery about what happens inside a real working agency. "Is it like the show *Mad Men*?" people would ask. Well, not really. Working at an ad agency is like working at any other company. There are some fun parts and some boring parts. But every now and then, something magical happens.

I'm a big NFL fan. And like everyone else in the country, I watch the Super Bowl on Sunday. Most years my team, the Philadelphia Eagles, doesn't make it to the big game (except for 2017 when they won their first and only Super Bowl). So usually, I'm not emotionally invested in the game, but I always love watching the ads. During all those years grinding it out in the ad industry, I never produced an ad that aired in the Super Bowl. However, I did work on one ad that was supposed to run in the game.

One of the GSK brands I worked on was Advair, an asthma drug. We were doing a campaign to promote asthma awareness, and NFL star Jerome Bettis (also known as "The Bus" because he would run over defenders) was our spokesperson. At the time, Jerome was the running back for the Pittsburgh Steelers, and it was his last season before retirement. We actually shot an ad with him promoting asthma awareness at Heinz Field, the home of the Steelers.

I had been pestering my clients that we had to run a Super Bowl ad featuring Jerome if the Steelers made it all the way. I remember watching the 2006 AFC championship game, the Steelers vs. the Colts. The Colts were the heavy favorite to win it all with Peyton Manning as quarterback. But the Steelers pulled off the upset and were heading to the Super Bowl.

So I texted my client: "Jerome will be the star of the most-watched event of the year. Should we buy a Super Bowl ad now?"

It was really a joke. I didn't expect much. But he texted me back a few minutes later and said, "Let's do it."

Wow. We just got approval to buy a Super Bowl ad. The only problem – we didn't have a "Super-Bowl-caliber" ad to run.

The next morning I talked to Rich Russo, our creative director. Rich is one of the best guys I've worked with in my career. Amazing creative talent, highly strategic, a strong manager/leader, and great with clients. I told him we had to produce a Super Bowl ad.

You have to realize that most companies spend a full year working on Super Bowl ads. We had less than two weeks. Rich spent a few hours coming up with ideas. In the afternoon, he walked into my office and said, "I got it!" He showed me a script for an ad that was a take-off of the classic Coke Super Bowl ad with Mean Joe Green from 1979. It was very appropriate because Bettis was a Steeler, just like Mean Joe.

We pitched the idea to our client. They loved it, and we were off to the races. In just a few days, we cast the spot, found a location, booked Jerome, and got a director. We also bought the media placement, so there was no going back.

Interesting note, the ad cost about $750,000 because we had committed significant media dollars to ABC Network that year, and they had available inventory in the game. Very few advertisers ever pay the full rate card for a Super Bowl ad. We shot the ad at Carnegie Mellon University on their football field. It ended up being a snowy day, which added a nice visual effect to the ad.

In the end, we were able to get it done. But right before we were going to ship the ad to the network, I got a call from my client. We had to pull the ad.

There had just been some recent PR backlash about pharmaceutical advertising in the press, and the senior executives at GSK were concerned about doing an ad in such a high-profile venue. It was a reasonable decision to make, but we were all devastated, including my clients.

Advertising is a tough business and requires a lot of resiliency. We all moved on to the next project. We didn't get our money back for the Super Bowl ad, but we were able to reallocate those dollars into other ABC programming. If you want to see the final ad, you can still find it on YouTube – just search for "Jerome Bettis Asthma Commercial."

Personally, I really like the ad, but I think it turned out just a bit schmaltzy. We originally had a humorous ending where the kid throws Bettis the jersey, then shakes his head and sarcastically says, "Super Bowl ads." After a lot of debate with our client, we ended up going for a more "emotional" ending. I still like the ad a lot, but I would have loved to have seen it run in the big game. Maybe next time...

Key Career Lesson: Advertising is a tough business and requires a lot of resiliency.

Launching Howard Stern

Of all my time in advertising, nothing compared to my experience pitching Howard Stern. One day I was sitting in my office when an email came in from our COO, Annette Stover, with the subject: "Are there any Howard Stern fans in the office?

I immediately perked up. I grew up outside Philadelphia listening to Howard on 94.1 WYSP. I actually remember when he came into the market and took on John DeBella, the hometown DJ on 93.3 WMMR, who had a popular show called "The Morning Zoo." Eventually Howard took over the #1 spot and came to Philly to hold a faux funeral for the "Death of DeBella."

I wouldn't call myself a Howard superfan. But I had been a listener for a long time, read his books, and saw his movie *Private Parts*. So I replied to Annette, saying that I'd be interested in learning more. She asked me to join a meeting later that day to get briefed by the marketing director from Sirius Satellite Radio. Our agency had been invited to pitch an ad campaign that would promote Howard's move from terrestrial radio to Sirius.

Wow! Do an ad campaign for Howard Stern? I had spent my entire advertising career doing ads for laundry detergent, snack foods, and pharmaceuticals. This struck me as an incredibly exciting opportunity.

I attended the briefing. It was pretty straightforward: Create excitement for Howard's move to Sirius and drive up subscriptions. The catch: We only had about two weeks to do the work. And we would be presenting directly to Howard and Sirius CEO Mel Karmazin. It was a pretty crazy situation.

So we got to work. The marketing problem was not insignificant. Howard had a large base of passionate fans who would follow him wherever he would go. Those fans went out and bought Sirius subscriptions as soon as Howard announced that he was leaving terrestrial radio. The real challenge was to convince the casual Stern fans to pay for something they were used to getting for free.

Dave Arnold and Jason Kreher were the creatives assigned to the pitch. They were both young, highly ambitious, and very good at doing work that was funny and smart, so they were the perfect team for the assignment.

When I briefed them, we talked about what made Howard, Howard. Yes, he was the "King of All Media." Yes, he was a "shock jock." Yes, he had millions of loyal fans. But what really made Howard interesting and compelling was the fact that he would always cross the line. He would push further than any normal person would, and that created great radio. There's a scene in the movie *Private Parts* where the radio station executive (known as "Pig Vomit") reviews listener research about Howard. Here's the exchange:

Researcher:	The average radio listener listens for eighteen minutes. The average Howard Stern fan listens for – are you ready for this? – an hour and twenty minutes.
Pig Vomit:	How can that be?
Researcher:	Answer most commonly given? "I want to see what he'll say next."
Pig Vomit:	Okay, fine. But what about the people who hate Stern?
Researcher:	Good point. The average Stern hater listens for two-and-a-half hours a day.
Pig Vomit:	But... if they hate him, why do they listen?
Researcher:	Most common answer? "I want to see what he'll say next."[15]

That dialogue captures the brilliance of Howard. He's compelling. You don't just want to listen, you have to listen. Because you know that if you're not listening, you'll be missing something.

---

15. *Private Parts*. Paramount Pictures, 1997.

So Jason and Dave set out to create advertising that was true to the brand. Advertising that would grab your attention. Advertising that you simply couldn't ignore.

The team developed several creative concepts that were really funny. But we didn't want to just walk into the pitch with storyboards on foam core, we wanted to blow them away. So we produced a series of videos that would showcase our creative talent and our understanding of the Howard Stern brand.

On the day of the pitch, we walked into the Sirius boardroom to get set up. We only had 30 minutes for the pitch, so we had to be brief and brilliant. No long setups. No strategic frameworks. Just the ideas.

Howard and Mel walked into the room. We did brief introductions and then got to it. (Interesting note, Howard is known as being extremely germophobic. He often talks on the air about how he hates shaking hands, so I instructed our team not to shake Howard's hand. But when he walked in, he came up to each one of us and shook our hands.)

It was surreal sitting there next to Howard and Mel. We showed the first video, and Howard burst out laughing. We nailed it. The meeting was a huge success. But a good meeting doesn't always mean you're going to win the business.

We waited. A few days later, I got an email from the marketing director at Sirius. She said, "Hi. Can you guys be down here at 2 pm today for a meeting? Welcome to the team."

I remember running around the agency like a maniac yelling to anyone who would listen that we won Howard! It was a great feeling. We went on to launch a lot of the work we had presented in that pitch.

Not surprisingly, a lot of the ads created controversy and had to be pulled. That ended up being a good thing because the PR value it generated was much greater than the media spend. One of our ads only ran in movie theaters showing rated "R" movies. And it still got a lot of complaints and was eventually taken down.

In the end, Howard's move to Sirius was a big success. He brought millions of subscribers to the company. He was a big reason that Sirius was able to acquire rival XM radio and create a single satellite radio provider. Looking back, I don't know how much the advertising campaign really contributed to the success, but as a Stern fan, I'd like to think it did help a bit.

I still look back at that pitch with great memories. It's one of those crazy stories I'll always remember from my New York ad agency days.

> **Key Career Lesson:** When you have a deep understanding of the brand and the target audience, you can do really great creative work.

Volvo: Innovative Creative

Fresh off my Howard Stern win, I got tapped to run Volvo's digital business. This was a great opportunity to work on a big iconic automotive brand. Volvo also had a reputation for doing really innovative creative work.

When I joined the team, the Volvo client wanted me to spend a lot of time in their Irvine office, so we agreed that I would be there every other week. Every other Monday, I would take a cab to Newark Airport and jump on the early Continental Airlines flight to John Wayne Airport in Santa Ana, CA. At the time, I didn't mind the travel much. Paige and I were married but didn't have kids yet. She had a full-time job at American Express that kept her busy during the week. It was fun living a bicoastal life with one week in NYC and one in Irvine. It's the kind of thing you probably only want to do when you're young.

My Volvo clients were very focused on innovation. We did a cool movie tie-in with the *Pirates of the Caribbean* film that featured an online puzzle game that had a cult following. We also produced the first-ever scripted comedy web series for the launch of the Volvo C30 that ran on MSN. The show starred Craig Robinson, who would later become a big-time comedic actor with major roles in *The Office* and the movie *Hot Tub Time Machine*.

I was really enjoying my work on the Volvo account. I had built strong relationships with the client, and we were doing work that was generating a lot of buzz in the industry. It's incredible to think that just a few years before, I was unemployed and living with my parents. My career was on track, and the future was bright.

AutoTrader

Life Happens

Then life happened. Paige was pregnant with our first child, and that made us reevaluate everything. Would we stay in the city? Should we move to the 'burbs? Would Paige keep working after she had the baby?

Anxiety levels were running high. One weekend we looked at two-bedroom apartments in the city, but it would be almost twice the cost of our one bedroom. That just didn't seem doable.

It was the first time we started talking about moving out of the city. That was a hard pill for me to swallow. I loved living in New York, but I also loved the idea of being a dad and building our family. I knew we'd probably have to leave the city eventually. I was just hoping it would be later rather than sooner.

Around this time, I got a call from a recruiter about a job opportunity in Atlanta with AutoTrader.com. It was interesting. I liked working in the automotive industry from my time on the

Volvo business. And AutoTrader offered a chance to go from the agency side to the client side for a fast-growing business, something I was very interested in.

Plus, we knew Atlanta very well from our time in business school and still had a lot of friends there. I did one of those online cost-of-living calculators to compare New York to Atlanta. It showed that if I could make a similar salary in Atlanta to what I was making in New York, essentially, it would be like doubling my salary. That would give us a lot of flexibility. Paige wouldn't have to work if she didn't want to. I could support us on my income.

I ended up getting a good job offer from AutoTrader, and they were going to pay to relocate me. I accepted. We packed up our small one-bedroom apartment, said our goodbyes to NYC, and headed back to Atlanta.

Key Career Lesson: Sometimes a change in your personal life can lead to unexpected career opportunities.

Riding the Digital Wave

The job at AutoTrader turned out to be a great experience. The company had started in the late 1990s and grown rapidly. When I joined, we were doing about $400 million in revenue and had almost 2000 employees. The marketing department alone had 100 people on staff.

AutoTrader was riding the digital wave. As companies took their advertising online, AutoTrader was perfectly positioned to grab a significant share of that spend. In the past, car dealers would spend big dollars on local TV and newspaper ads. AutoTrader had a simple proposition: put all of your dealership inventory online in front of in-market buyers 24/7 for a low cost of $3000 a month. Compared to traditional media, that was a great deal, and the company seemed to have unlimited growth potential.

I joined the customer marketing team, focused on our B2B program targeting car dealers and auto manufacturers. At the time, this was a new team. The marketing department had traditionally focused all its resources on consumer marketing to drive traffic to the website. As the company was entering a more mature phase, it needed to retain its customer base and improve customer satisfaction.

Many aspects of the job were extremely fun. There wasn't a lot of foundation in place when I took over the team, so I got to build the function from the ground up. I also learned the importance of collaborating closely with the sales team. (You can read more about this in **"Play Nice with Others" on page 81**.)

During my five years at AutoTrader, the company grew from $400 million to $1 billion. It was a great ride. There were some challenges for me though – my style never quite meshed with the organization, and I had a pretty tough relationship with some of the senior-level executives.

Nevertheless, I know I made a significant impact in my role. I had grown my team from four to fifteen. I took on a lot more responsibility in the company that expanded beyond just the marketing department. I built out the B2B function with successful campaigns, programs, and capabilities that were not there when I arrived.

In the end, there wasn't a clear path up for me at AutoTrader. I was stuck in a middle management role. In my mind, the higher up you go, the bigger impact you can have on the company. And that's what I was most interested in.

Key Career Lesson: If you can't move up in the organization, sometimes you have to move out to get the opportunity to advance your career.

PGi: A Key "Sucking Less" Story

I landed my first VP of Marketing role at a company called PGi, also known as Premiere Global Services. PGi was a really interesting company. Boland Jones founded it in 1991 as a company that did calling cards for the military. Over time and through many acquisitions, it got into the audio conferencing business. During its peak in the 2000s, it was a billion-dollar public company, driven by the significant demand for conference calls in enterprise companies.

As new technologies emerged, PGi's audio business started to decline, so the company rapidly pivoted into the web conferencing space. That's around the time I joined. PGi is one of the key drivers for the title of this book, because when I showed up, things weren't great from a marketing perspective. But they did get a lot better over time. Or, one might say that they "sucked less."

PGi gave me everything I could want in my first VP role. I had a lot of responsibility and a big team. I had the opportunity to make a big impact on the business, whether it was rebranding the company or driving significant SaaS revenue for our new web conferencing product. I got to do it all.

Unfortunately, that legacy audio conferencing business was an anchor holding us down. We had several hundreds of millions of dollars tied to that part of the company, and it was continually declining. We would see large enterprise customers churn, moving to other less expensive conferencing options. The focus on sustaining our dying audio business ended up taking our focus away from growing the more profitable SaaS web conferencing business.

While companies like Zoom only had to worry about selling web conferencing, PGi was a public company that had to split its attention and resources between the high growth SaaS solutions and legacy audio products. The lack of focus ended up being our downfall. PGi was acquired by private equity in 2017. Almost everyone I knew there is gone.

Looking back on my PGi experience, it still bothers me that we weren't more successful. We had such a good team. When you look around at many of the top corporate leaders in Atlanta and beyond, you see many people who have PGi on their resumes. I still stay in touch with many of them, and we often help each other when we can with advice and recruiting needs. So while we didn't hit it big with PGi, the experience does hold a special place in my heart. And it positioned me well for my next move as the CMO of QASymphony.

> **Key Career Lesson:** If your company doesn't have the right product and isn't focused, it's going to be a struggle.

QASymphony: A CMO Rocket

I've never been a person solely focused on my job title, but I will say it was pretty cool when I got the offer letter from QASymphony that said "Chief Marketing Officer." I had gotten to the top level of my function, and I was excited.

QASymphony was a fast-growing startup company that had just raised a Series A. They were scaling the company for future growth, and Dave Keil, the CEO, was building his team. I was introduced to Dave through my friend Sangram Vajre, who had passed on the opportunity to join another Atlanta startup called Terminus.

When we met, Dave and I bonded over our New Jersey roots and our mutual love for Bruce Springsteen. Dave was very excited about QASymphony's potential. The company was competing in the software testing space, one that had been neglected by many of the large players in the industry.

Hewlett-Packard had the dominant software in the category, called "Quality Center," but for years they had rested on their laurels and not released any software updates. It was old software that didn't play well with a lot of the modern tools agile development teams were using, like Atlassian's JIRA. As a result, testers were slowing the process and creating a bottleneck.

The QASymphony solution, called qTest, was similar to HP Quality Center in many ways, but it was built for agile development and integrated with JIRA. We were getting significant traction in the industry as large enterprises started to switch from Quality Center to qTest.

I had a great three-year run at QASymphony as we grew the company from $1 million ARR to $20 million ARR. Compared to a declining business like PGi, this was a rocket ship. During my time, we raised a Series B of $5 million and a Series C of $40 million. I had never been part of a fundraising process before, and I really enjoyed it. It gave me a chance to show potential investors how our marketing program was driving quality leads and revenue for the business.

The Series C created a lot of buzz in the Atlanta tech scene and, as the CMO, there were a lot of interesting opportunities starting to come my way. I guess when people see that you have success with one company, you become a hot commodity.

I really enjoyed my time at QASymphony. I had been part of the core team that built the business from the ground up. I loved the people I was working with. But there was one aspect of the job I didn't care for – the category. Software testing is a particular niche. And while I clearly understood the value we were providing to the tester, it was hard for me to get truly passionate about the product because I really wasn't a user. It was actually the first time in my career I was working on a product that I would never use.

For many people, this might not matter, but I enjoy working on products that I use every day. As more and more interesting opportunities presented themselves, I realized I was ready for a change.

> **Key Career Lesson:** It's important to have passion for the category or industry that you work in.

The ParkMobile Opportunity

One day I got a call from Leigh Segall, the CMO of Smart Communications. I had known Leigh for many years, from back when she was working at SAVO and I was her client at AutoTrader. Leigh has become a part of my peer network in Atlanta and someone I often turn to when I'm thinking through things.

Leigh said a company called ParkMobile was looking for a CMO. I had heard of ParkMobile before but didn't even realize it was an Atlanta-based company – and after being around the Atlanta tech scene for over ten years, I was very familiar with most of the major players in the market. I looked at my phone and realized that I had the app, so I guess I had used it at some point in the past. The company just clearly hadn't made much of an impression on me. But ParkMobile was doing something really cool: enabling people to skip the meter and pay for parking on their mobile device. I was immediately interested in learning more.

Leigh introduced me to Andrew Hamilton, the CTO of ParkMobile. Leigh and Andrew were on the board at the Technology Association of Georgia (TAG), and Andrew had asked Leigh if she knew anyone for their CMO search.

Andrew and I had a call to discuss the opportunity. It sounded really interesting, but there was one red flag for me. The company had a recent CMO who had only lasted six months. That's usually not a great sign. But the job checked a lot of other boxes on my list, so I thought it would be worthwhile to continue the conversation.

Andrew connected me with the CEO, Jon Ziglar, and we had an interview at the ParkMobile office in Midtown. Jon and I immediately connected. Like many CEOs, I could tell he was very intense but also had an excitement and optimism about the potential of the business that was very appealing to me. He made the point to me that today, ParkMobile is a parking app, but the future vision is much bigger. Just like Amazon started with books, ParkMobile started with parking but has ambitions to get into all aspects of consumer mobility – tolling, transit, EV charging, in-car apps, etc.

It was a great pitch and got me excited about continuing the conversation. I also liked the idea of working on a business that had both a B2B and B2C component. In my career, I'd always done one or the other. ParkMobile presented an opportunity to do both.

Jon asked me to put together a short marketing plan to present to the executive team. Some people hate doing these kinds of "homework" assignments. It's hard to be smart about a business where you don't have insider knowledge. But I actually like it. From my days pitching new business in the agency world, I learned how to put these kinds of presentations together to get potential clients excited about working with us.

For ParkMobile, this would be a similar exercise. I needed to demonstrate a high-level understanding of the business and the problems it needed to solve. Then I would provide some ideas on how to solve the problems.

As part of the presentation, I did some informal research with friends about the ParkMobile app. Everyone I talked to absolutely loved the concept, but most had never heard of it. Even more interesting was that several people who said they'd never heard of it actually already had the app on their phone and didn't realize it!

To me, the solution was clear. ParkMobile had very low brand awareness, even with people who had already downloaded and used the app. We needed to build the brand so people understood there's a better way to pay for parking.

One of the issues I immediately identified was the tagline: "Parking Made Simple." The word "simple" is problematic. Generally, people don't want simple solutions. Simple is basic. Simple is a Fisher-Price toy.

What do people want? Smart solutions. They want a smart car like Tesla or a smart thermostat like Nest. My recommendation was to immediately change the tagline from "Parking Made Simple" to "A Smarter Way to Park."

It was a pretty bold move in this kind of interview to come to the table and recommend changing the tagline. But I wanted to show them how I think and give them an idea of the changes I would like to make if I got the job. It was important to me that they understood that they were not hiring someone who would maintain the status quo and make some minor optimizations to the current program. If they chose to hire me, they would be hiring someone who would make major changes to the company's marketing program.

And this was a program that needed an overhaul at the time. The company actually had two completely different brand logos on all the marketing materials. When they developed a newer one, they never made the transition away from the old one; so anywhere you'd see ParkMobile, you'd see two completely different logos. And the ParkMobile website – a website designed to promote the mobile app – was not responsive for mobile devices.

Needless to say, there was a lot of opportunity for improvement. In my interview, I tried to identify the marketing issues or gaps I observed and show how I would fix or fill them.

At the end of my presentation, the team had a chance to ask me questions. One of the interviewers asked me, "You've done a lot of great things in your career. Why would you want to work here?"

The way the person phrased it sounded to me like she was a bit down on the company. She might as well have said,

"Why would good people want to join this shit show?" At least that was the way I took it.

I told her, "Look, you guys have built an impressive business. You have millions of users, and you're in tons of cities. There's so much potential here. Now you need to build the marketing engine that will take you to the next level. And that's what I love to do. Building things. Help companies grow. It's my thing."

With that, we ended the interview. Jon asked me to come to his office. I said my goodbyes to the team and followed him out of the conference room.

When we got to his office, he looked at me and said, "Man, I am just blown away by what you presented." He made me the offer on the spot and said he would send the formal paperwork over later. I told him I was very excited!

A few weeks later, I joined ParkMobile as the CMO.

What has been great about ParkMobile is that I actually got to execute many of the ideas I presented during my interview. We consolidated the brand to one logo, changed the tagline to "A Smarter Way to Park," and today, I'm very happy to say the website is responsive for mobile devices.

At the time I'm writing this book, I am coming up on my four-year mark at the company, and we're still growing fast. We recently hit the 25-million user milestone, up from 8 million when I first joined. It has been a great ride and keeps getting better. In 2020, I expanded my role within the organization, taking over the product team in addition to my marketing responsibilities.

Today, people who work at ParkMobile would never ask a question like, "Why would you want to work here?" In fact, in the past few years, we've won several awards for being a "Top Workplace." As fun as it is to grow the business, it's equally satisfying to know that you've helped create a strong and healthy organizational culture. ParkMobile is not a company people have to work for; it's a company people want to work for and like to work for.

Key Career Lesson: Find companies where you can use your skills and experience to make the biggest impact possible.

And another thing...

So, now you probably know more than you ever wanted to about my career. But I hope you understand that any career is a long journey filled with twists and turns, highs and lows. At every step, you need to embrace the opportunities to learn and grow. Stay positive and keep pushing forward, even when things aren't going your way. And probably most importantly, find the job that's the right fit for you.

When I walked into Saatchi & Saatchi for my first day of work, I could never have imagined that I'd be where I am today. It has been a truly great ride. And it's not done. As I finish up this book, my career just took another interesting turn: I was just named the CEO of ParkMobile. Another new chapter begins. But I'll save that story for my next book – perhaps "How Not to Suck at Being a CEO."

Wherever you are in your career journey, I hope you enjoy the ride, and I wish you the very best.

EPILOGUE:
THE TAG MARKETING AWARDS

I walked into the Georgia Aquarium for the 2019 Technology Association of Georgia Annual Marketing Awards ceremony. Over the years, I had been to the aquarium so many times for so many different award ceremonies.

Having worked at companies with small marketing budgets, I've learned that awards are a great way to build awareness for your brand. I generally try to apply for as many awards as I can – Best Place to Work, Fastest Growing Company, Most Innovative Product, etc.

In all honestly, these awards really don't mean much. They don't determine whether you succeed or fail as a business. But hey, who doesn't like to get a nice trophy or plaque every now and then?

This time the ceremony was for an individual award – "Marketing Executive of the Year." I had been nominated for this award a few times before, but each time I'd lost. Even though it's always an honor to be nominated, it really isn't much fun to sit there at an event and get passed over for another marketer. It was starting to become a joke. I would tell people that I was "the Susan Lucci[16] of the Atlanta awards circuit."

When I was nominated in 2019, I expected a similar outcome. I sat at the table with several members of my team, anxiously awaiting the announcement so I could congratulate the winner and leave.

The MC took the stage. He said a few things about the nominees, then: "And the Marketing Executive of the Year award goes to..."

I took a deep breath and prepared myself to be disappointed once again. I gave myself an internal pep talk: "These awards really don't matter. You're crushing it at your job. The results speak for themselves."

Then it happened.

The MC said, "Jeff Perkins."

The room applauded. I went up on stage and accepted my Lucite trophy and said a few words. Unfortunately, I didn't expect to win, so I had nothing prepared. I had to wing it. I'd also had a few adult beverages, so I was pretty loose at this point.

Here's what I said: "Something I've learned in a 20+ year career is that my success as a marketer has very little to do with me and how smart I am, what education I have, and what experience I have. It has everything to do with the team that I'm surrounded with. Without the right team, these awards really mean nothing. So as much as this is an 'executive' award, I see this as an award for the whole ParkMobile team."

I meant every word of that. *It's all about the team.*

I headed back to my seat with a big smile on my face, and as I sat down at the table, everyone was congratulating me. One person asked, "How does it feel?"

I looked at the award and said, "Well, it doesn't suck."

---

16.   Susan Lucci was on ABC's *All My Children* for its entire network run. She was nominated twenty-one times for the Daytime Emmy Award for Outstanding Lead Actress in a Drama Series, but she only won once, after the 19th nomination.

RESOURCES

Marketing Resources

Below is a list of good resources for marketers to check out, and in the next section you'll find a glossary of common marketing acronyms. I'll continually update both of these lists on my website, **www.hownottosuckatmarketing.com**.

Online Resources

Association of National Advertisers (ana.net)

Large trade association for the advertising industry. Features tons of good content on a wide range of topics. Paid subscription required to access it.

Backlinko.com

Another great resource for SEO tips. Action-oriented and practical advice.

Chiefmartech.com

Scott Brinker has covered the rapidly evolving world of martech since the early days. This site is the ultimate resource to geek out on all things martech. Just make sure you have a magnifying glass when looking at the latest martech landscape chart.

Crazy Egg (crazyegg.com)

Crazy Egg shows you a visual heatmap of website interactions. This helps you understand what people are doing on your site.

Google Analytics (analytics.google.com)

Google Analytics will give you a ton of metrics to help you improve the performance of your website.

Google Digital Garage (learndigital.withgoogle.com/digitalgarage)

Google offers all kinds of training and certifications on their different advertising solutions. If you work in digital advertising, this is a critical resource for you.

Hubspot (hubspot.com)

Probably the most complete marketing resource library online. They have articles about everything marketing. They also have Hubspot Academy, which offers educational content and certifications.

Landing Folio (landingfolio.com)

Effective landing pages can drive big results for your business. Landing Folio shares the secrets on how to build pages that deliver.

Marketing Profs (marketingprofs.com)

Very high-quality, in-depth educational content. Be sure to subscribe to Ann Handley's MarketingProfs newsletter.

Moz (moz.com)

If you want to learn SEO, there is no better resource out there. Make sure to check out the one-hour guide to SEO.

Product Marketing Alliance (productmarketingalliance.com)

Essential resource for product marketers chock full of templates and examples.

ReallyGoodEmails (reallygoodemails.com)

If you're looking for email inspiration, ReallyGoodEmails has you covered.

SalesLoft (salesloft.com)

Excellent content hub around effective sales engagement programs and better sales-marketing alignment.

Setup (setup.us)
Need to find an ad agency? Setup provides excellent resources on how to do this, including a checklist, sample RFP questions, and much more.

Terminus (terminus.com)
Terminus invented Account-Based Marketing, and their resource center is packed with high-quality content for B2B marketers. Also, check out co-founder Sangram Vajre's books, *Account-Based Marketing for Dummies* and *ABM is B2B.*

Usertesting.com
Usertesting.com is a great resource that lets you get real user feedback on your site so you can understand what's working and what's not.

Peer Groups

The CMO Club (thecmoclub.com)
The top peer group for executive-level marketing leaders with local chapters in most major cities.

Marketing Growth Leaders (energizegrowth.com)
Executive peer group run by Lisa Nirell, author of *The Mindful Marketer.*

Pavilion (formerly Revenue Collective – joinpavilion.com)
A group for B2B marketing and sales leaders.

Peak Community (peak.community)
Marketing group started by Sangram Vajre, co-founder of Terminus. The group has executive and emerging leader sub-groups.

Thought Leaders

Seth Godin (sethgodin.com)

Seth is one of the top marketing thought leaders in the world. He updates his blog every day, and it's worth the read. His books and podcasts are also very good.

Matt Heinz (heinzmarketing.com)

Matt Heinz is one of the leading voices in B2B marketing. His website is full of helpful content. Also, check out his CMO Coffee Talk Slack community.

Dave Kellogg's Blog (kellblog.com)

Dave has a great blog focusing on marketing for startups and tech companies.

Neil Patel (neilpatel.com)

If you want more website traffic, Neil Patel has the content to help make that happen.

Joe Pulizzi (joepulizzi.com)

Joe is an expert in content marketing. His e-newsletter is a must-read.

David Meerman Scott (davidmeermanscott.com)

David has written several bestsellers on the "new rules" of marketing, sales, and PR. He's a keynote speaker at many of the top marketing conferences.

Gary Vaynerchuk (garyvaynerchuk.com)

Gary Vee has become an icon with marketing and sales professionals. He's a highly entertaining public speaker and his first book, *Crushing It*, is worth a read.

Podcasts

B2B Marketing Leaders Podcast (podcasts.apple.com/us/podcast/b2b-marketing-leaders/id1529489359)

Dave Gerhardt has engaging conversations with a range of B2B executives.

Brands, Beats, and Bytes (brandpositioningdoctors.com/podcast)

Podcast mixes marketing, tech, and culture with great conversations.

CMO Suite (thecmosuite.com)

Sean Halter hosts this entertaining podcast featuring CMOs of top companies.

Hustle and Flowchart (evergreenprofits.com/category/the-podcast)

One of my favorite names for a marketing podcast. Features interviews with a who's who of marketing thought leaders.

Renegade Thinkers Unite (renegade.com/podcasts)

Drew Neisser hosts this podcast focusing on B2B marketing leaders.

State of Demand Gen (refinelabs.com/podcast)

Podcast focused on practical tips for revenue marketers.

Glossary of Marketing Acronyms

These are some of the key acronyms I've talked about in the book. It's by no means an exhaustive list, but it covers some of the main ones you will hear often.

AIDA – Awareness, Interest, Desire, Action: A marketing framework used to define where the customer is in the sales cycle.

ABM – Account-Based Marketing: Marketing micro-targeted to a specific company.

B2B – Business to Business: Marketing activity targeting a business customer.

B2C – Business to Consumer: Marketing activity targeting a consumer.

B2G – Business to Government: Marketing activity targeting government entities.

BOFU – Bottom of Funnel: This means the customer has gone from the top of the funnel (TOFU) to the middle of the funnel (MOFU), and is now close to buying the product.

CAC – Customer Acquisition Cost: The total sales and marketing cost to acquire a customer.

CMS – Content Management System: A solution that enables a marketer to create, publish, and manage a library of content related to the company on a website.

CPC – Cost Per Click: The amount it costs to get someone to click on your digital ad.

CPC – Cost Per Conversion: The amount it costs to get a user to take a specific action (i.e., sign up for a demo, submit contact information, download an app).

CPL – Cost Per Lead: The amount it costs to generate a lead or contact for the business.

CPM, CPT – Cost Per Thousand: This is the cost an advertiser would pay to get 1000 impressions for an ad or campaign. (The "m" is for mille, which is Latin for one thousand.)

CPA – Cost Per Acquisition: The amount it costs to acquire a user as a customer.

CR – Conversion Rate: The percentage of leads converted at a specific stage or touchpoint in the buying process. Also used to refer to the number of people on a website that convert into a contact.

CRM – Customer Relationship Management: A software program (e.g., Salesforce, Hubspot, Sugar CRM, Microsoft Dynamics) that enables an organization to track engagement with clients and prospects.

CTA – Call to Action: The key message on a marketing asset that communicates what a person needs to do next. Examples: buy now, get a demo, schedule an appointment, learn more.

CTR – Click Thru Rate: Shows the percentage of people who have clicked on an ad or link compared to the number of people who saw it.

KPI – Key Performance Indicator: Key metrics that show the overall performance of a marketing program over time.

LTV – Lifetime Value: The financial value of a customer over the estimated lifetime of their engagement with the company. Also can be called Customer Lifetime Value (CLTV or CLV).

MOFU – Middle of Funnel: The customer is in the evaluation process for buying the product. The next step is to get the customer to the bottom of the funnel.

MQL – Marketing Qualified Lead: A lead that has been generated and qualified by marketing as viable for the sales team to follow up on.

NPS – Net Promoter Score: A customer satisfaction metric that measures how likely customers are to recommend your business to others.

PPC – Pay per Click: Digital advertising model requiring the advertiser to pay every time a person clicks on the ad.

PR – Public Relations: The promotion of a business to the public through various media channels. PR placement is earned through a relationship with a journalist rather than paid for (like advertising).

ROI – Return on Investment: The financial return a company will get on any investment made.

ROAS – Return on Ad Spend: The company's financial return on specific investments in advertising.

RON – Run of Network: A way of buying digital ads that will run across an entire publisher's network versus just one website.

ROS – Run of Site: A way to buy online ads from publishers that run your ads throughout the entire site versus a specific section or page.

RTB – Real-Time Bidding: A real-time auction of digital advertising inventory that enables a marketer to buy ads in real-time based on supply and demand.

SaaS – Software as a Service: Subscription-based software that companies use for various tasks (CRM, email, social media, etc.). SaaS products charge a monthly subscription which can also be paid annually.

SEO – Search Engine Optimization: The activity of making your web content accessible by search engines.

SEM – Search Engine Marketing: Leveraging search engines for marketing activities. Includes Search Engine Optimization (SEO), paid search ads, company profiles, photos, videos, reviews, etc.

SQL – Sales Qualified Lead: A MQL that has been vetted and qualified by the salesperson.

TOFU – Top of Funnel: The customer is just learning about the product. The next step is to get the customer to the middle of the funnel (MOFU).

USP – Unique Selling Proposition: The value proposition of the product/service to the customer that differentiates the offering from the competition.

UX – User Experience: The overall experience a customer has when interacting with a business at all the different possible touchpoints.

VTC – View Through Click: This means the user saw your ad, did not click, but eventually visited your website. This is an indicator that the ad was effective in influencing the user.

WOM – Word of Mouth: A marketing tactic that generates buzz where people talk to each other about the company.

WTF – What the F&@K: What you say when you see this long list of marketing acronyms.

Acknowledgements

Big thank you to everyone who helped make this book happen.

To the talented publishing team at How2Conquer: Emily Owens and Michelle Newcome, thanks for your faith in a first-time author and for gently guiding me through the process. You kept me organized and on schedule! To Telia Garner, for sprucing this book up with your fun illustrations and a kickass cover.

To John Brown, one of the authors of *A Dragon Walks into a Meeting*, for introducing me to the How2Conquer team after reading some of my blog posts and encouraging me to write a book. And yes, John, my book will outsell yours.

To the bosses, mentors, and role models who have been instrumental in my career journey – Jon Ziglar, Dave Keil, Scott Tapp, Boland Jones, Ed Trimble, Chip Perry, Rich Russo, Denis Budniewski, Kurt Lundberg, Marc Greengrass, Marie McNeely, and Claire Hassid.

To my awesome teammates, past and present, who have always lifted me up, made me laugh, and proved that the sum is greater than the parts – Jennifer Zember, Drew Prante, Reed Gusmus, Ryan Yackel, Gina Kawalek, Mark Lister, Olivia Batty, Kevin Graham, Allison Gilli, Brad Goldman, Donnie Senterfitt, Meghan Hilton, Joely Nadler, Katie Mahon, Allison Sitzman, and Katie Kennedy.

To my friends and colleagues who read the advanced copy of the book and provided valuable feedback – Jeff Crow, Alexandra Gobbi, Chad Gold, Jo Ann Herold, Drew Neisser, Kevin OMalley, Leigh Segall, Nicole Wojno Smith, Mike Steib, and Jennifer Zember.

To my parents, Rick and Shirley Perkins, who always encouraged me to do more writing when I was young.

And to my wife Paige, the best proofreader I know, who read through multiple drafts of this book and was always very happy to point out my many grammatical errors and typos. I could not have done it without you.

About the Author

With over 20 years of marketing experience, Jeff Perkins is a self-described marketing geek who frequently contributes to several marketing publications and speaks at many industry events. Jeff's work has earned him numerous accolades, including the Atlanta Business Chronicle's MAX Award for marketing excellence and the Technology Association of Georgia's Award for Marketing Executive of the Year.

Jeff is currently CEO at ParkMobile, but he started his career grinding it out in the NYC ad industry. His experiences range from traditional to digital, B2C to B2B, and agency-side to client-side. When he's not working, you might find him riding his Peloton bike or attending a Bruce Springsteen concert (he's been to 32 so far). He lives in Atlanta with his awesome wife, two adorable daughters, and two poorly behaved dogs.

www.ingramcontent.com/pod-product-compliance
Lightning Source LLC
Chambersburg PA
CBHW071600210326
41597CB00019B/3334